Fundamentals of Writing:
How to Write Articles,
Media Releases, Case Studies,
Blog Posts and
Social Media Content

Fundamentals of Writing:
How to Write Articles,
Media Releases, Case Studies,
Blog Posts and
Social Media Content

Paul Lima

Published by

Paul Lima Presents

www.paullima.com/books

Fundamentals of Writing: How to write articles, media releases, case studies, blog posts and social media content - First Edition 2013

Cover and interior design: Paul Lima. Copyright © 2013

Published by Paul Lima Presents
www.paullima.com/books

Manufactured in the U.S.A.
Published in Canada

ISBN: 978-1-927710-01-2

Contents

Introduction

Welcome to *Fundamentals of Writing*, a book written specifically for those who want to improve their writing skills and apply them to writing articles (for newspapers, magazines, corporate and other publications), media releases, case studies, blog posts and social media content. The book is based on several writing courses that I teach online for University of Toronto continuing education students and for private students and corporate clients.

Fundamentals of Writing is for you if you are looking to

- become a more effective writer;
- organize your thoughts before you write;
- write for a defined audience;
- make your points in a clear, concise, focused manner.

If you are like me, you fear the blank screen or blank page. You look at it and feel intimidated. You see it as an empty vessel you have to fill with words—only you are not quite sure which words to use, how to order them or how to use all those squiggles (known as punctuation marks).

Perhaps you are not like me. Perhaps you love the sight of a blank page. You view it as a blank canvas, an opportunity to create. However, you may feel your creations take too long to come to fruition. You start, you stop, you start again. Moving forward is a slow, painful journey, and you often feel you've missed your mark or destination, even if just by a tad, when you are done.

Welcome to the wonderful world of writing.

My hope is that this book will help you overcome that feeling of intimidation. And if you don't feel intimidated by the blank page, that's cool. My hope is that the book will simply help make you a stronger, more confident, writer. In both cases, the hope is that this book will help you write in a more focused and concise manner, and will help you effectively structure your written communication when writing articles, media releases, case studies, blog posts and social media content.

Although the book covers writing stronger sentences and more organized paragraphs in the last couple of chapters, it does not cover spelling or grammar or how to write advertising or promotional copy, business documents (email, letters and reports) or how to write for the web. (Visit www.paullima.com/books for books on most of those topics.)

When it comes to the fundamentals of writing, this book will get you grounded and focused—especially if you feel as if you're often spinning your wheels when you write. *Fundamentals of Writing* focuses on the writing process to get you thinking about your audience, purpose and desired outcome before you start to write. Then it helps you effectively and efficiently write well-structured, focused documents in a clear, concise manner. You will come to understand the importance of following that process no matter what you are writing because, simply put, writing is a process. To improve your writing, you need to understand the process and apply it in a dedicated and disciplined manner. Exercises in this book will help you apply the process to the types of writing previously mentioned.

The book will also help you spark your writing creativity and exercise your writing muscles, to get them into shape before you start to plunge into writing projects. And, as mentioned, there are a couple of practical chapters toward the end of the book that will help you improve your sentence and paragraph structure, should you need some help with your writing at that level.

Note: This is the first edition of the book. The book should be 99.5% error-free. If, however, you like to play "spot the tpyos," feel free to let me know if you find any, or have any other comments about the book. Email me—info@paullima.com.

Paul Lima

www.paullima.com

1/ The Importance of Creativity

Writing is considered an art by most fiction writers, one that involves a great deal of creative thought. For the rest of us—those who write business documents, articles, case studies, media releases, blog posts, social media content, web content and even non-fiction books—writing is a craft. However, even crafts involve at least a modicum of creative thinking, some types of non-fiction writing more than others, admittedly. Technical competency and understanding the structure of the document you are producing are important; however, unless you are producing a price list, it is difficult to imagine writing without a degree of creative ability.

With that in mind, we are going to look at some creative techniques and do several creative exercises that you may be able to apply to your writing, or at least use to loosen up before you start to write. But before we look at creativity and writing, let's look at something that can interfere with creativity, or what I call your internal critic or censor.

Writing seems to be painful in some way for almost everyone. For instance, when it comes to spelling and grammar, English is a convoluted and inconsistent language. For many of us, including me, spelling and grammar—let alone stringing words together in coherent sentences—can be frustrating. If you're my age, that frustration might include some early memories of grade school teachers who seemed to relish slashing thick red marks through your earnest writing efforts. For me, that would be Mr. Conron, my grade five teacher. As confusing as the rules are, having a teacher crush your work under the weight of red slashes can make the act of facing the blank page an intimidating endeavour.

My internal critic/censor, Mr. Conron, would not give me a pen in grade five, the year students graduated from pencil to pen. Instead, he made me use a pencil all year because I could not spell well or write neatly enough to earn my ink, so to speak.

But there was a reason for this.

Writing, to me, was complicated. All those rules and exceptions to them. Who could keep track? Maybe you, but not me.

It is "i" before "e" except after "c," isn't it? Oh, unless the word has an "aye" sound as in neighbour. If that is the case, how do you account for "weird"? When it comes to writing rules, that word is just ... well, weird. So my writing was messy because I could not spell! When you don't know if it's "i" before "e" or "e" before "i" you make a chubby "i" and a skinny "e" and put the dot right in the middle, hoping to fool the teacher, which I seldom did.

Mr. Conron wielded his red marker like the sword of Zorro, gleefully cutting huge red gashes across my mistakes. He never once commented on content or creativity. He just slashed at mistakes, as if perfect spelling and grammar are what writing is all about. There was no room for art or craft, just correct spelling and grammar. Oh, and neatness.

I battle Mr. Conron whenever I attempt to master the creative art of writing. When he rears his ugly head, I say, "Get thee behind me, Satan!" And I keep on writing—through typos and grammatical errors, through incomplete sentences and incorrect words. I write until I have finished an error-filled first draft and then I laugh in his face. Because I have learned something about writing: writing is a process. First, you create, and then you correct. Mr. Conron (and Word's automatic grammar and spell check) be damned!

Even before you create, there are steps you need to take to become a more effective and efficient writer. However, before we look at the writing process in detail, answer me this: You, too, have an internal censor. Who is it? Take a moment. Identify your critic/censor. Name him or her. Give him/her a nickname (like Satan). Place your thumb on the tip of your nose and wiggle your fingers at him/her. Go on. Do it. Say your critic's name (or names!) out loud and thumb your nose at your Mr. Conron ... There! Doesn't that feel better?

Now ... pick up a pen. Find a sheet of paper. And write about your internal censor/critic, and what impact he or she had (or didn't have) on your writing. Write without stopping or correcting yourself. Screw spelling, grammar and neatness. Just write, write, write. Write as if you were freefalling—falling from an airplane without a parachute. Nothing can stop you. Not grammar. Not spelling. Not Mr. Conron. Take five or ten minutes and write, write, write ... . Doesn't matter what you write or where you go. Just write…. Don't censor yourself. Consider this for your eyes only. Abandon your internal censor, and… On your mark ... Get set ... Write!

Write about your internal censor for 5 minute or so, and then read on.

How to Overcome Your Mr. Conron

Welcome back. Hope you are feeling okay… First, understand that writing is a *process*. Mistakes are part of the process. In the process, there is a time to *create* and a time to *revise*. If you do not follow the process, Mr. C. will trip you up every time. He will get you *revising* or *editing* when you should be *creating*. He will cause you to waste time editing work that is not even at the first-draft stage. He will have you feeling frustrated and stupid.

Writing is difficult enough without Satan squeezing the last ounce of fun out of what should be a challenging but enjoyable creative art or craft. I use several creative writing exercises to bypass my Mr. C. They help me focus on the creative aspect of the work and even get a document organized or outlined before I start to write. I save dotting the *i*'s and crossing the *t*'s for the last stage of the process—editing—and relegate Mr. C. to a small (but important) role as *editor*. In short, I lock him in a cupboard, feed him nothing and only use him when I need him. And I do need him; every writer needs an editor. But there is a place for him in the process, and it is not when you are getting organized or creating.

Before we look at right brain, or creative, exercises in this book, here are a few words for thought you might want to think about:

"It took me my whole life to learn how to paint like a child again."
– *Pablo Picasso*

"Never look at a reference book while doing a first draft. You want to write a story? Fine. Put away your dictionary, your encyclopaedias, your World Almanac and your thesaurus … . You think you might have misspelled a word? Okay, so here's your choice: either look it up in the dictionary to make sure you have it right—and break your train of thought—or spell it phonetically and correct it later. Why not? Do you think the word is going to go away? When you sit down to write, write. Don't do anything else except go to the bathroom, and only do that if it absolutely cannot be put off."
– *Stephen King*

Do you see what these words are saying? When you are creating, you must overcome your inhibitions and internal censors. You must be as free as a child. In short, *when you are creating, spelling and grammar do not count*. There will be time for correcting later, once you have completed a first draft. After all, who do you show the first draft to? (*To whom do you show your first draft?*) Nobody! Who cares if there are *tpyos*? Fix them later.

If you are working in a word-processing program like Word and you have your spell checker and grammar checker turned on, you are inviting Mr. Conron to inhibit your creativity. You are seeing and correcting so-called mistakes as you write—before you complete your first draft. In doing so, you are wasting time and losing your creative train of thought. Brainstorming, pre-writing exercises and the first draft are for your eyes only.

With that in mind, *turn off spell check and grammar check and start creating.* Try these exercises below using pen and paper, unless otherwise indicated. There is something formal about neat rows of letters and words on the computer screen. They just seem to cry out for revision when you should be focused on creation! So use pen and paper for the creative exercises.

Writer's Journal

Since you will be writing while reading this book, I suggest you start a writer's journal, using either a notebook or a specific file on your computer. Whatever the case, it should be an easily accessible place where you can write as you work your way through the book.

Your writer's journal is where you write notes, observations and reactions, and the place where you do your journal exercises. It is your safe place. It is not a diary. It is you playing in your "creative" sandbox. It is not for public consumption. So have fun in your journal, and don't censor yourself.

Does that mean anything goes in your writer's journal? To answer succinctly: yes! Why not? *It's for your eyes only.* Enough said.

In addition, you might want to write in your journal for fifteen minutes or so a day, at least three days per week—even if you think you have nothing to write about. Simply use what you learn—particularly from your freefall and clustering—and write about it on a regular basis in your journal.

Again, your journal is not a diary. Keep notes in it and use it to practice some of the exercises you will read about over the next few chapters. In other words, don't just try the exercises once and move on. Try them while you are reading the book, and then make them a regular part of your journal-writing practice or workout.

When is the best time to write in your journal? Whenever you can! Perhaps you can take time first thing in the morning or just before going to bed, or instead of watching the news. Only you can find, or make, time to write. And if you want to be a writer, writing when you don't necessarily have anything to write about is a great way to exercise your writing muscles and clear your head so you can clearly focus on what you have to write about when you have writing work to do.

Right-Brain Writing and Pre-Writing Exercises

Below are several right-brain (creative side of the brain) pre-writing exercises that will help you tap into the creative side of writing. While you may not need to use each of these exercises before you write, using them is a great way to exercise your writing muscles before you engage in the more serious endeavour of trying to write a document. Just as a sprinter or marathon runner would not run a race without a regimen of exercise and without warming up, these exercises will help you get into writing shape and can be used to warm up before you write.

Also, if you suffer from writer's block, these exercises are a great way to unblock writer's block. (They are such great ways to unblock writer's block that I have written a more extensive writing exercise book called *Unblock Writer's Block*. The book presents these and many more writing exercises in detail.)

In addition, when conducted with a particular topic in mind, the exercises presented here can help you discover ideas, themes, words, phrases and other material that will make it into your document, so they are a great way to conduct internal research—to look for material you can use in your writing.

Freefall

Freefall has been called "writing without a parachute" or "stream of consciousness" writing. Freefall is a means of writing whereby you literally write, for five minutes or so, without stopping. When you freefall, you don't have to have anything in particular to write about. You just put pen to paper (recommended over fingers to keyboard) and write, write, write. You don't stop, no matter what. Think of yourself as an artist practicing gesture sketching (rapidly drawing and playing with lines or "gestures" that do not necessarily become pictures). There is no goal or destination. You start without a beginning and do not have to end anywhere in particular. Just jot down the first thought that pops into your mind, followed by the next and then the next and then the next ... .

In other words, to sustain your freefall, tap into your stream of consciousness—the thoughts that are flowing through your mind (even as you are reading this page, you can hear them rushing through your mind)—and write, write, write. If you feel yourself coming to a halt, doodle or use ellipsis (...) until you tap back into the stream. Do not stop.

Do not stop to correct spelling, grammar or punctuation.

Do not stop to reflect upon or edit your work.

Do not stop.

Write quickly, without stopping to edit or revise.

It can feel unusual to write when you think you have nothing to say, or to continue to write when you know you have made a spelling or grammatical error. However, that is the whole point—to get used to the separation of writer and editor by jumping into the stream and letting the current take you somewhere, anywhere, or nowhere in particular. Just follow the stream of consciousness as it meanders through your mind. Write without censoring yourself, until you reach what feels like an end. Or not. Give yourself at least five minutes, if not more.

Journal Exercise: Let's Freefall

I want to stress here that your freefall does not have to be a straight narrative. Have fun. Play. Experiment. Push your personal boundaries. If you latch on to something that feels like a bit of business writing or work-related writing, run with it. But do not try to impose form or narrative on your freefall. Write fast. Do not pause. Especially do not pause to revise.

What I suggest that you do now is this:

- Sit comfortably where you will not be interrupted for the next while.
- Write for at least five minutes; if you can, set a timer for five minutes.
- Pick up your pen, start with whatever is flowing through your mind and keep on going.
- Don't stop until your time is up.

If you are not ready to freefall, take a break. But don't put off starting for too long. When you are ready…

…Begin your freefall.

Once you have written a five-minute (or so) freefall, continue to read.

Freefall Purpose

Now that you've done your first freefall, you may well be thinking, "Is there a purpose to it?" Is there a point or purpose to all the gesture sketches an artist does, the voice exercises an opera singer does or the stretching a runner does?

This is your warm-up. This is you getting in shape. This is you learning to write for the sake of writing. This is you in a no-pressure, not-for-publication situation discovering the joy of writing—even if it feels like a pain. This is you separating the writer from the editor. This is you learning how to become a more efficient and effective writer.

Journal Exercise

I encourage you to do this exercise daily to help you loosen up and write quickly. You might even want to freefall before you start reading each chapter. However, since you are new to freefall, please try one more—before you read on. Get comfortable, set your timer and…

…Begin your freefall.

Once you have written your second freefall, continue to read.

Directed Freefall

Directed Freefall works like freefall, only you are given (or produce) an opening line to help direct your creation. However, as with freefall, there is no goal or destination. Simply write as freely as possible, without censoring yourself and see where your writing takes you.

You can find directed freefall "beginnings" or opening lines almost anywhere: a sentence in a newspaper, book or report; a snippet of overheard conversation; something you hear on the radio; something you read on the web… The opening line sometimes imposes structure on your writing or leads to you writing a narrative passage. But not always. Sometimes it inspires. But not always. Sometimes it is a relief to have somewhere to start. Sometimes it makes you feel shackled. The point is to use the first line as a starting point and freefall, no matter how you feel.

Journal Exercise: Directed Freefall

So take five minutes or so, and try a directed freefall using the line below. If you are not ready to freefall, take a break. But don't put off starting for too long. When you are ready…

…Begin your directed freefall starting with the following line:

It took a long time to…

Once you have written a five-minute directed freefall, continue to read.

Here are a several other opening lines that you can use to kick-start your directed freefall:

- In the beginning was ... .
- On the day that I was born....
- In the old woman's face, I saw ... .
- It all ended the day ... .
- In the town where I grew up....
- It came upon a midnight's eve....

The goal is to have fun, to play, to create for the sake of creating, to write without revising. So pick a line. Jot it down, and freefall from there. Take five minutes and do nothing else but write, write, write ... . When your freefall seems to have come to an end, pick another line and go again...

Once you have written a couple of directed freefalls, continue to read.

Freefall hint: Before you begin writing anything important, freefall for five minutes or so. It helps clear the mind so you can focus on your task. Also, you might find inspiration related to your work. But even if you don't, the process of clearing your mind will then help you focus.

Clustering

Now we're going to try clustering, a form of brainstorming (also called mind mapping or word association). Clustering lets you brainstorm in a visual manner. When clustering, you jot down (using a specific method) all the words you *associate* with a given topic, key word or phrase. The goal is to get down on paper all you know and associate with your key word. Once again, work quickly—without censoring yourself. That means you might jot down some words or phrases that seem "silly." For instance, if your key word is "agriculture" and one of the words that comes to mind is "Batman," that's not a problem. Jot it down and keep on clustering. You never know where these so-called silly words will lead. So, whatever comes up, goes down!

How Do You Cluster?

Here is what to do when given your keyword or phrase:

- Jot it down in the middle of a blank page, underline it and circle it.
- Draw a short line (more like a long dash) from your keyword and jot down the first word or phrase that comes to mind.

- Circle that word or phrase (optional).
- Draw a short line from that word or phrase, and jot down the next word or phrase that comes to mind.
- Repeat until you come to the end of the cluster string of associated words (in other words, until you go blank).
- Return to your keyword.
- Moving quickly, draw a short line from your keyword and jot down the next word or phrase that comes to mind.
- Circle that word or phrase, draw a short line from that word or phrase and carry on ... .

How many cluster strings should you create? It is up to you. The goal is to move as quickly as possible, without censoring, so you can get down as many words or phrases as possible that you associate with your keyword.

Why do you do this? Because it beats looking out the window waiting for inspiration to strike.

Clustering and freefalling are active methods of inspiring creative ideas. Also, as you will see, solid ad copy contains words and phrases related to the concept or hook behind the ad. You are, in effect, mining for words and phrases that will help you develop your ad theme.

If your concept (keyword) appeals to your target market, so will many of your cluster words. Used in ads, words that appeal to your target market are like landmarks. They help the target market identify with the product or service you are advertising and keep the target market interested or engaged in your ad.

Speaking of *target market*, what do we mean by that term? Target market is an advertising term that, quite simply, describes the market the advertiser is targeting. In your case, you will be targeting readers. There are several ways you can identify your target reader based on the publication (print or online) you are writing for. Your target reader could be based on demographics (age, gender, income and so on), lifestyle, sector the reader works in, position within a company, type and size of company, and so on. No matter what you are writing, or whom you are writing for, you want to keep your reader in mind.

Below is an example of clustering based on the key word "clustering." Review the sample before you try a few of your own based on the key words provided.

Journal Exercise: Clustering

Below is a key word that I'd like you to use for your first cluster. Get a blank sheet of paper, jot down your key word and then cluster for five to ten minutes. Keep your mind open and your censor at bay…

…Begin your clustering starting with the following key word:

Heart

Once you have clustered for five or ten minutes, continue to read.

Journal Exercise: Clustering II

Let's try one more before we move on. Below is another key word that I'd like you to use for your second cluster. Get a blank sheet of paper, jot down your key word and then cluster for five to ten minutes. Keep your mind open and your censor at bay...

...Begin your clustering starting with the following keyword:

Writing

Once you have clustered for five or ten minutes, continue to read.

Journal Exercise: Clustering Continued

Here are several other keywords you can use to keep on clustering, now or later in your journal:

- Me
- Apple
- Help
- Writing
- Summer (or any season you wish to use)
- Money
- Chocolate
- Spider
- Mother (or Father or any sibling)

I'm sure you can come up with dozens of words or phrases you can use as keywords. Before you read on, try clustering several times using a couple of the words above or words of your own. Cluster for about five minutes each time, or work until your clustering exercise feels complete.

Take some time, if so inclined, and produce a couple of clusters before you read on.

Cluster/Freefall Combo

Clustering is an excellent pre-writing exercise. It can be used to fuel your freefall. Once you have completed a cluster (a cluster is complete when it feels as if it is finished), flip into freefall, and write without stopping. However, if you find yourself slowing down or running dry as you freefall, glance quickly at your cluster to spark your writing.

Journal Exercise: Clustering/Freefall

Using one of the words above or below, try a cluster/freefall combination:

- Home
- Mother
- Blue sky
- Last night
- Hunger
- Travel
- Fear

Notes on Clustering

You can use clustering to help you write anything once you have defined the *type of document* you are producing, *your target audience* and *your purpose*. For example, what you produce when clustering the word "Me" would change in relation to the *type of document* you are producing, *your target audience* and *your purpose* for each of these documents:

- Autobiography, childhood reminiscence or personal essay
- Business bio for a website or speaker's introduction
- Cover letter and resume

Could there be some overlap in your clustering? For sure. But given a direction (by defining the type of document you are producing, your target audience and your purpose) your clustering will shift into the appropriate gear. That doesn't mean you force it or censor yourself. It just means once you know where you want to go and why, you are more likely to go there overall with your cluster.

Try multiple clusters for one project. Before writing a cover letter or resume, for example, cluster *Me*, *Education*, *Work Experience*, *Hobbies*, *Passion*, *Career Objective* and *Job Title* (the actual title of the job you are applying for). Apply the results of your brainstorming to your cover letter and resume. Clustering these key words will also help you prepare for your interview.

Journal Exercise

Are you working on an article or other document? If so, pick a keyword that represents what you have to write and cluster it. Then flip into freefall. See where it takes you.

Before you read on, take ten minutes or so to try a cluster using the word ME and flip into freefall. See where you go with it.

Clustering Comment

While I can't guarantee that clustering will work for you when you have something to write about, I encourage you to try it several times before your next writing projects. You can cluster as soon as you have an assignment to help you get focused on what you have to write about and to help you determine what you know and need to know about the topic. And then you can cluster once you've done your research to help you get your thoughts down on paper. Clustering can work well. It can help you get organized before you write, which will help make you both a more effective and efficient writer.

Allow me to quote an accountant who was taking a business-writing seminar in which I introduced clustering. I confess, I thought the accountant, a senior partner at the firm, would find clustering a bit too new age and perhaps even kind of airy fairy or artsy fartsy. But he went along with my request to cluster a work-related word. He chose to cluster a key word that he associated with a major report he was writing for his firm.

To this day, I can still quote what he said after completing his clustering:

You freed one gigabyte of RAM. I was holding it all in and you had me pull this information out of nowhere. Everything I need to know is down on paper. Now that I know what I'm going to say, I have brainpower left to think about how I'm going to say it. It's all over but the writing, and the writing is no longer intimidating.

He said this before moving from clustering to creating an outline. In other words, he saw in his spider's web of words everything he needed to write about. Once he had all the topics down on paper, it was a matter of organizing the information by creating his outline (more on that later), and then writing his report—from outline point to outline point.

Practical Clustering Application

Clustering can be applied to any writing. If you research a topic, you can cluster a key phrase associated with it before you write. Examine your cluster and you might find a natural outline. Organize the outline and fill in the blanks, so to speak, before you write a first draft.

I once had to write a report about establishing a continuing-education computer-training department for a college. After a great deal of research and several meetings where many opinions were expressed, I sat down to write ... and found myself blank. I was on information overload and could not think straight. So I clustered:

Computer Education Centre

Clustering helped me put on paper all issues, costs, benefits, and challenges that had been discussed in various meetings and other reports. The cluster allowed me to create an outline with sub-points under each heading. Then, all I had to do was fill in the blanks.

Four hours later, the first draft of the report was complete. Yes, I had to go back to some of the research I had done to get prices, projections, and other details, but I knew where in the report this information was to go.

Whether you are writing articles for periodicals or documents for corporate clients, clustering can help you work faster, more efficiently and even more creatively. It's what you are paid the big bucks to do.

Try it. You might be amazed at how well it works.

2/ Communication Process

Communication is a process that often, but not always, ends with feedback. If you want to communicate effectively—in writing or when speaking—you should understand the communication process.

Communication requires a *sender* who sends a message through a *channel* (email, letter, report, article, tweet, blog post and so on) to a *receiver* (the reader). The process is not complete, however, without *feedback*. Feedback closes the communication loop. Sometimes, *noise* (competing messages, distractions, misunderstandings and so on) interferes with your message. Feedback lets you know if the receiver understood your message.

Again, you don't always need feedback. If you are writing an article for a publication, you seldom solicit feedback. You might, however, if you are writing an editorial or writing for a publication that advocates social justice and wants people to participate in the political process. The main thing is to be aware of the communication process so you can make conscious decisions about how to use it.

Advertising and Feedback

When you communicate in person, you can ask for feedback if you want it. You can ask people if they understood what you were saying or if they have any questions. However, when you communicate in writing or other one-way media (such as broadcast, which is primarily speaking the written word), it is more difficult to ask for feedback.

Advertisers want feedback when they communicate so they can measure the effectiveness of promotions, and they have learned how to use direct-response marketing techniques such as discount coupons, time-limited offers, and so on to motivate people to take action, such as buy something or request more information. They then measure the received feedback—how many widgets were sold, how many people called for more information or, these days, visited a website. If an advertiser doesn't know how effective its promotion was, how will they know whether they should run the same ads again, modify them, or scrap them and come up with something new?

In business writing, if you do not close the communication loop, how will you know if the desired action has been or will be taken by the person or group of people you have written?

Again, you do not have to ask for replies from everybody you email or to whom you send information or from everybody who reads your articles. In many instances, your writing purpose might not require you to close the loop, especially if you are writing news articles for publications or websites. In business, you often send messages "FYI"—for your (the receiver's) information. In other words, no action required. Again, the key is to know before you write if you want feedback, and how it should be taken if required. That way, you can work a call to action into your document—buy now, call today, storm the barricades at 3:00 PM, send a letter of protest.

If you want to know if the recipient has taken the requested action (or has any questions), you need to close the communication loop. You can ask for a reply and monitor the situation to see if action has been taken.

In advertising, as mentioned, and often when using social media (Twitter, Facebook, blogs, and so on), you go one step further: You not only ask for action to be taken, you try to motivate it.

"Save 20% if you buy before November 30" is an attempt to motivate someone to buy a product by a specific date. If sales go up, you have your feedback and know your motivation worked.

"Click here to read about the new Filibuster 300 and receive 10 free tips on…" is an attempt to motivate a click. "Blog post on <topic>. Read and enter to win. Click here <website address>," goes the tweet. Without getting into web analytics here, I want you to know that you can monitor clicks to your ten free tips or contest after you send out your promotion, and you can then gauge your feedback or how well your promotion did.

Again, if you do not require a reply (literally a reply or feedback or action), then you may not need to close the communication loop. Deciding whether to close it or not should be a conscious decision, based on your particular needs. The important point here is this: if you need to know that the receiver has received and understood your message or taken a particular action, then you have to put into place a method of closing the communication loop. If the loop does not close in a timely manner—timely as dictated by you and your circumstances—then it is your job to troubleshoot the process. In other words, you can assume that your message has been received and understood or you can build feedback into the communication process so you know it has or you know if you need to follow up.

Understanding the need to close, or not close, the communications loop or to motivate, or not motivate, action can make you a better writer, but only if you can write well and structure your entire document to lead up to the call to action (or conscious lack of one).

3/ Pleased to Meet You

While you need to understand the communication process to decide if you will or will not attempt to solicit feedback, you also need to understand the writing process so you can organize what you want to say and how you go about producing anything you write.

The writing process is different than the communication process. It is the approach you should take before you write, as you are writing and once you have completed writing a document. It is the process you follow when writing anything, be it an email, an article, a media release, a blog post or even a 140-character tweet.

Following the process, outlined in detail in the next chapter, will make you a stronger, and more confident, writer. How you apply it, and how much time you spend on each aspect of it depends, in large part, on what you are writing, your target audience or primary reader and your purpose.

While this process can be applied to any non-fiction document, and even to some works of fiction, our focus in this book will be on applying the writing process to articles, media releases, case studies, blog posts and social media content.

But first, before we get to the writing process, I'd like to meet you—three times.

Journal Exercise: First Introduction

Before you read about the writing process, I want you to take a moment and pretend you are introducing yourself to me. Write your introduction any way you like.

Take some time now, before you read on, and write your introduction to me.

Once you have written your first introduction, continue to read.

Journal Exercise: Second Introduction

I now want you to write a second introduction. This time, we are going to prepare using *who, what, where, when* and *why* (and sometimes *how*)—known in journalism as the *W5*. Before we look at how you would apply the *W5*, however, let's look at a few of the things you need to know before you begin to write almost any document:

- Word count or page length
- Due date
- Audience and audience's expectations
- Purpose or objective

Since it is an introduction, not a book or a report, it should not be too long. So we have word count more or less covered. If you are a stickler for exactness, though, let's say your introduction should be from twenty-five to sixty words in length. We know this version of your introduction is due before you complete this chapter, since I will be asking you to do it soon, as part of this chapter. So we have a due date of sorts.

As far as audience is concerned, you can pretend you are going to send it to me to show me a sample of your writing and to introduce yourself to me. With that in mind, as your reader or audience, what do you think I need from you? In other words, what is my expectation? Do I want your life history, or do I simply want to know *who* you are and *what* you do in relation to *why* you purchased this book? Although the former might be an interesting read, will it be a practical read? The latter, on the other hand, is what you might expect me to want to know.

Finally, what is your purpose (*why*) in writing your introduction? Let's assume you want to tell me why you bought the book and what you hope to get out of it—how you hope it might help you. With that in mind, I want your second introduction to answer the following questions:

Who are you?

What do you do (or hope to do)?

Where did you buy this book?

When did you buy this book?

Why did you buy this book?

Before you write your introduction, answer the above questions in point form. Then review your points and determine which ones you'd want to use in your introduction. How do you determine that? Think of who I am and who you are, my (the reader's) expectations, and your purpose for writing the introduction. Eliminate any points that don't make the cut, write your second introduction based on the ones that do, and revise it as may be required.

Once you have written your second introduction, continue to read.

What Did We Do?

Consider the writing of your second introduction as an introduction to the five-step writing process. How so? Let's look at what we just did:

Preparation

- Defined the audience
- Determined the expectations of the reader
- Defined the writer's purpose

Research

- Conducted internal research by answering the W5 questions

Organization

- Organized the document into a rudimentary outline (when you eliminated points you did not want to cover)

Writing

- First draft

Revision

- Edit and proofread

The preparation, research and organization should have helped you focus your document on your reader and your purpose, as well as eliminate any points that did not relate to your reader or purpose. Therefore, you should have a more focused and concise document that makes sense to the reader and helps you achieve your purpose.

Shouldn't any document be both focused and concise? Shouldn't it make sense to the reader and help the writer achieve a predefined purpose? That is what following the writing process does to your writing—it makes it focused and concise. As a reader, I suspect you appreciate focused and concise writing. That does not mean you can't enjoy a long, rambling read. That means such reads are inappropriate when writing articles, media releases, case studies, social media content and business documents.

Journal Exercise: Third Introduction

So are we done introducing? Maybe. Ask yourself a few things: how long is your introduction and what person did you use? Did you use first person (I, me, my, we, us) or third person (he, she, they)?

While business correspondence can be in first person, it is often in third person. And most of the documents we are going to work on in this book also tend to be written in third person. (We will look at exceptions as we progress through the book.) Sometimes the choice of which person to use is subjective. For instance, I have chosen to use third person on my website (www.paullima.com) to promote my business writing and business-writing training services. Here is a variation of what you'd find on my website:

Do you require clear, concise, focused case studies, media releases, blog posts, website and/or promotional copy? With 20+ years of business writing and promotional writing experience, Toronto freelance writer and copywriter Paul Lima delivers the right words, on time and on budget.

Do you want your staff to write clear, concise, focused email messages, proposals, reports, web content and other documents? As a qualified business-writing trainer, Paul can train your staff to write effectively and efficiently.

The distance of third person can lend objectivity and a greater degree of credibility to a document. In addition, bios are often written in third person—perhaps to appear on a website or to be read by someone who introduces you before you make a presentation or give a speech. Third person also gives you a sense of distance from yourself. That sense of distance can help you revise your work to ensure it is as focused, complete and concise as it should be.

There are times when using first person is perfectly acceptable and even preferable. For now, though, I want you to review your second introduction. If it uses first person, I want you to write it one more time, in third person. Even if your bio is already in third person, make sure the content and length is appropriate for the occasion—introducing yourself to the author of this book.

What the author would want to know about you, the buyer of the book, and what you would want the author to know. If your bio is more than five sentences or more than sixty words long, reduce it to no more than five sentences or sixty words. In this way, you will more formally experience revision, the final step in the writing process.

Once you have written your third introduction, continue to read. If you want to introduce yourself to me, feel free to email your introduction to info@paullima.com.

4/ The Writing Process

As indicated in the second journal exercises in the previous chapter, there are five steps in the writing process:

- Preparation
- Research
- Organization
- Writing
- Revision

As you read about the process, you might find yourself thinking that if you have to go through the entire process every time you write something, it will take you forever to write anything. However, the time required to complete each step varies depending on the nature of the project. For instance, if you are a subject matter expert, you might not have to spend any time on external research. If you write a particular type of document regularly, you might not have to spend much time on preparation; you might even have a template you fill in each time you write.

When writing an article, case study or media release, however, you will spend much more time preparing, researching and organizing. You might even have to produce a formal outline (an integral component of organization) for approval before you start to write. As you write, you might discover some gaps in your knowledge and have to conduct more research and incorporate new material into your outline. When you complete your first draft, you will probably spend considerable time revising to ensure that your writing is as clear, concise, and focused as it can be, and that all points covered in the work reinforce your purpose or reason for writing.

You might have to send your document to an editor or a superior, or even a committee, for feedback and approval. The person reviewing the work will most likely make suggestions and send it back to you for revision. That is to be expected and is all part of the process when someone has to approve your work before it goes out the door.

Effective and Efficient

Let's say that following the writing process means you will spend a bit more time producing a document. Allow me to ask you this: Would you rather take a little longer to write a document that achieves what you want to achieve, or take less time and not achieve your purpose? I presume you would rather do the former. If you do not achieve your purpose when you communicate, what's the point of communicating?

Having said that, I believe that following the writing process will make you a more effective *and* efficient writer. Most of us get hung up on correct spelling and grammar before we even complete a first draft. That inhibits the process. Spelling and grammar count (although writers sometimes break the rules for effect). But spelling and grammar are the last elements of the process. Efficient writers spend time planning (preparation, research, and organization) before they write. They allocate time for editing (revising and proofreading) after they have written. This leads to producing effective documents—documents that achieve specific purposes. Or, as one University of Toronto study found:

Efficient writers spend 40% of their time planning (preparation, research and organization), 25% writing and 35% revising.

Less-efficient writers spend more time overall on projects and distribute their time differently: 20% planning, 60% writing (tinkering, writing, tinkering), and 20% revising, tinkering, revising.

Less efficient writers don't plan what they want to write and end up with less satisfactory, or less effective, results. It may seem counterintuitive to say that you can become more efficient if you spend more time planning. However, the time you invest up front in preparation, research and organization pays dividends when it comes time to write.

Think of writing as a trip. If you plan your trip, you are less likely to get lost and more likely to arrive on time. That does not mean you cannot meander as you travel. You can. However, if you meander and your side trip takes you nowhere, you will find it easier to get back on track because you have a road map or, in the case of writing, a process that includes a detailed outline.

Writing Process in Detail

Although we've looked at an overview of the writing process at the beginning of this chapter, I want to take a bit of time to more formally review each component of the process.

Before you start to write, you should understand the full process so that you can apply the process to various documents in this book. Having said that, there may be times when you can take short cuts and there may be times you spend little or no time on some aspects of the process. But before you take short cuts, you want to ensure you understand the full process.

Preparation

- Establish your primary purpose.
- Assess your readers (or audience) and their expectations and awareness of the issue(s) about which you are writing.
- Determine the detail into which you must go to achieve your purpose.
- Select the appropriate medium for delivering your words.

Research

- Determine if the research will be internal, external, or a combination of both.
- Find appropriate sources of information.
- Take notes and document external sources.

Organization

- Select an appropriate method of development so that your writing unfolds in a logical manner.
- Prepare an outline, breaking your document into manageable chunks.
- Consider your layout, design, and visuals (illustrations, graphs, charts), if responsible for them.

Writing

- Write from outline point to point, using each point like the opening line in directed freefalls; expand each point into sentences and/or paragraphs.
- Write with spell check and grammar check turned off.
- Complete a first draft, or a full section of longer documents, before revising.

- Spend time on getting the opening (called the lead or lede in articles) right, before moving on; in business documents, such as reports or proposals, you will often write the introduction and executive summary last as those document components summarize the body of the document and you can't summarize what you haven't written).

Revision

- Revise with the reader and subject matter in mind to ensure the tone is appropriate for both.
- Revise to ensure your document is clear, concise, and focused and supports your purpose.
- Check spelling and grammar.
- Peer edit if possible.

Note about Research

This book does not go into detail about research, but I'd like to make a couple of comments on the topic for you to consider. There are two types of research: internal and external.

Internal research. If you possess all the required knowledge, interview yourself before you write! In other words, if you are a subject matter expert, you can simply jot down on paper all you know and all you need to know about the subject or the product or service you are writing about. If you are knowledgeable, but have some knowledge gaps, jotting down what you know and need to know will help you identify knowledge gaps to help focus any required external research. Clustering is, as you have seen, is a great way to get down on paper all you know about a particular topic and speed up your writing because you don't have to stop and recall everything you want to write about as you write.

External research. If you do not possess all the required knowledge you need to write about a topic, you can interview yourself before you write (clustering helps you do this) to identify knowledge gaps before you start your external research. (As someone who has written literally hundreds of articles on numerous topics for scores of publications, I know what it feels like to have huge knowledge gaps.) Once you've identified knowledge gaps, you can then focus your external research so you can fill those gaps.

You can conduct background reading online (although you want to make sure you are reading credible websites; never take everything you read on Wikipedia at face value) and at libraries. You can also fill your knowledge gap by conducting interviews with subject matter experts (such as academics, researchers or others who are knowledgeable about the topic you need to write about).

Writing

Before writing a document, I suggest you choose a title or a working title. Even if the document doesn't require a title (a tweet for instance), it's good to have a topic line or phrase in front of you that encapsulates what the document is focused on, and why. Your title or topic line might change after you've written your document, but it will help anchor your writing as you write your first draft.

Once you start writing your body copy, follow your outline, which we will look at in the next chapter. Write swiftly from outline point to outline point until you have completed your first draft and before you do any editing.

Take a break after you produce your first draft and before you edit. If you are producing a long document, take a break after you complete each section, or several sections, of the document. You won't lose your train of thought if you have a detailed outline in place; it lets you know where to start when you return to the document.

Revision, Editing, Proofreading

Edit your documents after you have written your first draft. To help edit your document, ask yourself a couple of questions. Have I captured the purpose of the document using language that appeals to the target reader? Does the document unfold in a logical manner that is easy to follow? Is each paragraph well structured? Is each sentence well structured? Is the document clearly and concisely written? If you answer "no" to any of these questions, edit your document.

Once the document is as well written as possible, proofread it to correct any typos—spelling or grammatical errors. Printed documents can be more easily proofread than documents on a computer screen. If, however, you are like me and you don't want to waste paper (or you want to save the trees) you can best proofread your work on screen by reading it out loud. Also, increasing your document's font size (and reading it out loud) will help you catch those little errors.

Learning from Advertisers

Finally, although this is not a copywriting book, there are things you can learn from advertisers: in particular, the degree to which copywriters get to know their readers before they start to write and how and why they structure documents to AIAA (capture *attention*, hold *interest*, influence *attitude* and call for *action*).

Advertisers get to know their target audience (or target market) intimately before they produce advertisements. They conduct research and produce ads that meet the expectations of a well-defined demographic (gender, age range, income level, education level and so on). Sometimes they hold focus groups to get into the heads of their target market so they can produce ads that meet psychographic expectations. (Psychographics describes consumer groups based on psychological or emotional traits, characteristics or lifestyles.)

While you may not need to know your audience as intimately as someone producing advertising or marketing material does, you can still learn from advertisers, in particular from the headlines they use to capture the attention of their target audiences.

Look at how the two headlines below define their target market. The second one might not be apparent at first, but it does define its target market, as you will see.

Headline: Over 40? Acne Blemishes?

The headline is marketing an acne product for adults. Notice how it cuts through the clutter of all the other acne medication ads out there by clearly defining its target market: If you are under forty, then this ad is not for you; if you are over forty but have a clear complexion, then this ad is not for you; if you are over forty and have acne, then this ad is for you.

The headline captures attention by clearly defining its target market and creating an expectation in the reader. The reader expects to find a solution to his or her acne problem.

If the rest of the ad copy does not quickly deliver on the implied promise of a solution (in other words, demonstrate how it will meet the created expectation) it will fail to hold the interest of the reader. If it does not hold the reader's interest, it cannot influence the reader's attitude—to believe the product will work, for instance. And if the ad does not influence the reader's attitude, it cannot motivate the reader into action—in this instance, to buy the product.

I am not asking you to write advertising copy, at least not in this book. (If interested in writing ad copy, see my copywriting book, *Copywriting that Works!*) I am asking you to apply the advertiser's thought process to your writing. That thought process can be summed up in four letters: AIAA, as you will see in the section below the next headline.

Headline: Take a Walk on the Mild Side

Let's get inquisitive. What product or service do you think this headline is promoting? From what has this headline been derived? Is there anything familiar about this headline? Does this headline engage you? *Who* is the target market for this headline? *Why*? *What* is the target market's connection with the product or service promoted? *What* is the purpose of the ad?

Many people think the product is a mild salsa, and I don't blame them. It could be, but it's not. The headline is actually promoting a walk to raise funds to help find a cure for Alzheimer's disease. If you are familiar with the 1972 song, Take a Walk on the Wild Side, the headline will sound familiar to you and you will know the headline has been derived from, is a play on, the song. If you are a boomer who came of age in the early 1970s, then the headline will engage you. You will read the headline and start humming. That is engagement.

Now think of the service—a walk to raise funds to help find a cure for Alzheimer's disease. While boomers are not suffering from Alzheimer's in great numbers, they are starting to suffer from it. In addition, many of them have seen their parents go through it. While some boomers might do this walk, that is not the intent of the ad. Boomers are the target market for this headline because they are most likely to donate to those who do the walk. They've seen their parents suffer from this debilitating disease and they will contribute in the hope that a cure can be found before it has an impact on them.

AIAA: Attention, Interest, Attitude, Action

You may not think you are *selling* when you write, but if you want your reader to take a specific action, come to a particular understanding or even make up his or her mind about whatever you are writing about, you need to sell the reader. To do that, you need to do what advertisers do:

Attention: Capture the attention of your reader and set expectations

Interest: Hold reader's interest by demonstrating how you will meet relevant expectations

Attitude: Change or influence your reader's attitude

Action: Call for specific action

Depending on what you are writing, you "AIAA" by doing the following:

- Capture your reader's **attention** by using appropriate titles and sub-titles, subject lines, opening lines and/or paragraphs, and/or executive summaries.

- Hold your reader's **interest** with clear, concise, focused writing that reinforces the reader's beliefs and expectations, or enlightens the reader through the presentation of relevant information.

- Influence or change your reader's **attitude** by overcoming any objections your reader might have, informing the reader of the benefits of your position, product or service, and by stating your case in a logical, persuasive manner—supporting your arguments with relevant facts.

- Achieve your purpose by defining the **action** you want your reader to take and asking your reader to take it by a specific date, as may be appropriate.

In summary, to be an effective business writer, you must AIAA so you can sell your purpose—the reason you are writing. Again, you may not believe that you are in sales, but if you want somebody to do something, believe something or "buy into" something or agree with something, you have to sell that person on the action (be it agreeing, signing a petition, attending a protest, or making a major purchase) you want taken.

If you are writing an objective article, you need to present all sides of an issue for the article to appear objective. If you are writing a service article—why it pays to be fit or how to make a good first impression on a job interview, for example, you want to convince the reader that being fit or making that first impression is important before you can tell (sell) the reader on how to do it. In other words, as the reader, I still need to know what you are writing about, why it's something I'd be interested in, and how to do it. Miss any of those ingredients, and your article falls apart. And, of course, the article has to show up in a publication or on a website where readers care about whatever it is you are writing about. So the writing process and AIAA all work together.

In short, you are most likely reading this book because you want to become a more effective writer. The communication process, writing process and AIAA are the foundation of effective writing. Before we become more effective writers (and, I hope, more efficient ones too), however, we have to get organized. Let's see how clustering can help you conduct internal research and can facilitate the outlining or organizing process.

5/ Outline Before You Write

Organization is the third step in the writing process. Following preparation and research, organization is what you do before you start to write. Before you start to write sentences and paragraphs, you get organized by creating an outline. But where do you find the words, phrases and lines that become your outline? In your cluster. As mentioned, it does not hurt to use clustering as soon as you have a subject to write about because it can help you figure out what you know, and what you need to know, about the subject. But once you have completed your research, you should cluster again to help you organize your thoughts. The spider's web of thoughts you produce when clustering can help you create a detailed outline. Then you write from outline point to outline point until you have completed your first draft.

Writing-Related Cluster

Before we look at formal outlines, what I'd like to do is this: think of a key word or phrase that you associate with an article, media release, case study, blog post, social media content or anything else you want to write about. If you have nothing to write about, feel free to pick a topic you have previously written about. In other words, I want you to pick a topic that you know something about—a topic on which you have already conducted some research or know a fair bit about.

The key word or phrase you use in this exercise should be something that defines or summarizes the topic. Don't worry too much about the exact wording. Once you have that key word or phrase in mind, I want you to spend a few minutes thinking about your audience (*who* are they; *why* would they be interested in this topic; *what* do they know, not know and need to know about it?). Also, think about your purpose: *Why* are you writing about this topic? *What* do you want the reader to do, if anything, or think, if anything, or understand, if anything?

Journal Exercise: Clustering

Once you have spent some time thinking through the above, you are ready to cluster. (**Note:** If you find yourself screaming inside, "This is going to take me all day!" take a deep breath. We are going through the process in a fairly meticulous manner. You will get faster the more you do it.)

So, with your key word or phrase in mind, write it down, underline it, circle it and start clustering.

Once you are ready, begin clustering using…

<Your Key word>

**Cluster your key word or phrase as extensively as you can.
Once you have completed your cluster, continue to read.**

Journal Exercise: What Now?

Once you finish clustering, here's what you do:

- Take a highlighter to your web of words and highlight any words and phrases (topics) that you think you should write about in your document.

- Place the topic words or phrases in priority sequence (the order in which you think you should write about them) to produce a rough outline of your document.

- Review your draft outline and revise it as required based on your subject, purpose and audience. Also keep in mind the scope of the document—short article, feature article, media release, case study, blog post, social media content, for instance, or short email message versus a proposal or report if you are working on a business topic. As you revise it, eliminate any points you don't need to cover and fill in any gaps with new points you might think of.

You don't have to do anything more for now. We will soon look at how to create a formal outline.

**Highlight words or phrase and jot down those you might write
about, in the order in which you might write about them,
before you continue to read.**

Creating Outlines

I hope you can see how clustering can draw information out of you, and how producing an outline, even a rough one, based on your clustering means that you don't have to start writing with a blank page. (If not, do try clustering your key word again, or pick another word or phrase and retry the exercise.) Instead, you can start to write with an outline before you, which is kind of like having a series of directed freefall opening lines in front of you.

To write your document, you simply freefall from outline point to outline point. The more detailed your outline, the less you have to hold on to as you write, and the more effectively and efficiently you will be able to write a concise, focused document.

But before you start to write, you want to convert your cluster-based outline into a complete, detailed outline. This should not take too much work. Here's what you do: review your cluster-based outline and revise it—put the topics in the order you think you should write about them, delete any points you feel you will not need to write about, add any points that may be missing.

Again, your final outline should be based on your purpose, audience, scope (the degree of detail expected by your audience or required to achieve your purpose) and the nature of what you are writing. A media release tends to be one page. A feature article can be two thousand to five thousand or more words. A blog post may be two hundred to six hundred words. A tweet is only 140 characters. The longer and more complex the document, the longer the outline. And no, you may not outline your tweet, but that does not mean you don't follow the writing process and think about your topic, audience and purpose, and any desired action (as we shall see) before you write it!

Why Create an Outline?

Does this feel like work? Most people think it does, and there is a valid reason for the feeling. It is work. But what's the alternative? You can, of course, try to fill the blank page off the top of your head with words that will make sense to your audience and help you achieve your purpose. But guess what happens when you try to do that? Your brain tries to write well—to write coherent, well-constructed sentences and paragraphs produced in a logical order—and to spell correctly and follow the rules of grammar. And, as it is trying to do all of that, it tries to keep track of what you have written, what you are writing and what you still need to write.

Now your brain is a remarkable organ; it can do all of that, and more (although there are days my brain seems to do none of that and less). What I am suggesting you do here is relieve your brain of some of this workload by creating an outline—a formal list of all the points you need to cover placed in the order you feel you should write about them.

An outline brings focus and logical order to your document. It liberates your brain and lets you concentrate on writing each point in a clear, concise, focused manner. Your brain won't have to remember what you have written while thinking about what you are writing and what you still have to write. If you follow the writing process, which lists editing as the final component, you also free your brain from thinking about grammar and spelling on the first draft.

Think of it this way: For long documents (say two thousand words), you can pound on the keyboard and attempt to fill ten blank pages with words, sentences and paragraphs that make sense and unfold in a logical manner. Or you can produce ten major outline points and write ten shorter sections. Which seems simpler to you? But why stop there? Why not produce ten major outline points and several sub-points per major point, and then write in even shorter chunks?

With all this liberated brainpower available to you, you can focus on making your writing as effective as possible. And isn't that your primary goal—to write as effectively as possible?

More on Creating Outlines

Once you have your points on the screen in logical order, you convert them into more detailed points or even into sentences, and create a more detailed or formal outline. Below are a couple of outline examples. The first is a major topic outline on the subject of creating outlines. The second is a more detailed outline on the same topic. The major topic outline includes the subject you are going to write about and, in this case, sets out the two major topics you are going to cover:

Creating outlines

- How to create an outline
- Benefits of outlining

To create a more detailed outline, you would add sub-points below the major topic headings, as in the following example:

How to create an outline

- Outline major topic points
  - Subdivide topic headings where appropriate
  - Further subdivide subcategories if appropriate
- Benefits of outlining
  - Provides logical structure
  - Helps you detect errors in logic

o Gives you a detailed road map
o Lets you meander, if you wish, without getting lost
o Removes the stress of trying to hold onto all you know about a topic while you are writing about it
o Makes you a more confident writer
o Ensures all major and minor points are covered, in order
o Produces greater clarity and focus
o Allows you to write quickly in manageable chunks
o Ensures you do not lose your train of thought when you have to take breaks from writing; give examples
o Facilitates the approval process, if approval is required
o Lets you write from an approved outline
o *Should* minimize revisions by superiors or editors

Benefits of Outlines Expanded

Can your outlines be even more detailed? Absolutely. The greater the scope of the document (in other words, the longer the document), the longer and more detailed the outline should be. I'll show you a longer outline shortly; however, first let me address some of the points listed under "Benefits of outlining" in the outline above.

Outlines provide a logical structure to your document. If you have brainstormed all the points you need to know and listed them in the order that you want to write about them, then you can detect errors in logic. I don't know about you, but I'd rather revise a series of outline points before I start to write than revise an entire report several times because my writing did not flow in a logical manner.

Also, if you have a detailed road map to follow, it will get you from point A to point B in the shortest possible time. Instead of weaving all over the writing road and heading down dead ends, you'll start where you should start, take the route you need to take, and end up where you want to be. (Notice how that last sentence was not in my "benefits" outline. But notice also how it is related to and logically follows the "gives you a detailed road map" point. That is the kind of focused writing that an outline can help you produce.)

Does that mean you cannot meander? Of course not. If you think of a point that did not make it into your outline, you are free to explore it. If it is something you should write about, make room in the outline for it. If it is something that proves to be a dead-end, leave it out. The point is, even if you wander, the outline will ensure that you don't get lost. It will keep you on track, ensuring that you cover all major and minor points, in an order that makes sense to you, to your topic, and to your reader.

A detailed outline means you do not have to hold on to all you know about a topic while you are writing about it. That removes a great deal of the stress that you might otherwise feel while you are writing and helps you write with greater confidence. If you are covering all the major and minor points you need to cover to convey your purpose or achieve your goal, then you will write with greater clarity and focus.

With an outline in place, you can write quickly in manageable chunks. Instead of having to write a fifteen-page report, you only have to write a series of chunks or sections. That also reduces the stress associated with writing. And it ensures you do not lose your train of thought when you have to take breaks from writing. For instance, if the phone rings, you can finish a sentence, take the call and then pick up your writing at the next outline point. Or you can go home at the end of the day knowing you will come back to the document the next day and pick up where you left off—because the next point you want to address is there in your outline.

If you have to get a major document approved before you can distribute it, send the outline out for approval first. The person who has to approve the document can see if you have covered in your outline all the points you need to make. If any points are missing, or if the approver does not think your points are as logically structured as they should be, then she can add (or delete) points or move them around before sending the outline back to you. When you start to write, you will be writing to an approved outline.

That does not mean the person who has to approve the report won't make some changes; however, the changes are more likely to be of a subjective nature rather than a request to revamp and reorganize your entire document. I know, however, that some people who have to approve documents will ask you to revamp or reorganize anything you've written, even if you have carefully followed the approved outline. That's why my last points said "*facilitates* the approval process" not "*guarantees* the approval" and "*should* minimize revisions by superiors" not "*will* minimize revisions…"

Even Longer Outlines

As I have said, if you are writing a long report or research paper or an academic thesis or book, you will want to produce a long, detailed outline. (If you are writing a non-fiction book, you might be interested in reading my book, *How to Write a Non-Fiction Book in 60 Days*.) I'd suggest that you divide your outline into major sections or chapters. Beyond that, the premise is the same: outline major and minor topic points. Be as detailed as possible because the time you invest up front producing a detailed outline, will save you writing (and even revising) time.

In short, a section outline might look something like this:

Major topic of section (or chapter)

- Major point 1
  - Sub-point 1
  - Sub-point 2
- Major point 2
  - Sub-point 1
  - Sub-point 2
  - Sub-point 3
  - Sub-point 4
- Major point 3
  - Sub-point 1
  - Sub-point 2

It is, however, recommended that you include secondary, tertiary and other sub-points in your outline, such as this:

Major topic of section (or chapter)

- Major point 1
  - Sub-point 1
    - Secondary point 1
    - Secondary point 2
      - Tertiary point 1
      - Tertiary point 2
  - Sub-point 2
    - Secondary point 1
      - Tertiary point 1
      - Tertiary point 2
    - Secondary point 2
      - Tertiary point 1
      - Tertiary point 2
      - Tertiary point 3
  - Sub-point 3
    - Secondary point 1
    - Secondary point 2
      - Tertiary point 1
      - Tertiary point 2
      - Tertiary point 3

You keep on going until you have outlined every point in every section of your document (or in every chapter of your book). In short, following the formal outline process will get you to the stage where it is all over but the writing (from outline point to outline point). As any professional writer will tell you, that's a great place to be; however, you don't have to be a professional writer to get to that place.

Detailed Outline in Action

Do you want to see a more detailed outline in action? Look at the chapter headings for this book. They were all written before the text was written. Did the names of some of the chapters change as the book was being written? Yes. Did some chapters get broken in two? Yep. Were a few chapters shifted around? Actually, no. But it could have happened.

If that does not seem like much of an outline, look at the sub-headings in each of the chapters. They were almost all in place before I began to write. I produced the outlines (there were several outline drafts) after completing planning and research.

I had an outline but there were several digressions and meanderings as I wrote. A few led nowhere and were deleted. Others were incorporated into the text. So, an outline does not stifle creativity and improvisation. It allows for it.

Journal Exercise: Clustering/Outline

Think of another word or phrase that you associate with an article or other document that you are working on, or reuse the word or phrase you used in the last chapter. Once you have that key word or phrase in mind, think a bit about your audience (*who* are they; *why* would they be interested in this topic; *what* do they know, not know and need to know about it?). Also, think about your purpose: *Why* are you writing about this topic? *What* do you want to reader to do, if anything, or think, if anything, or understand, if anything?

Once you have spent some time thinking through the above, you are ready to cluster. So, with your key word or phrase in mind, write it down, underline it, circle it and start clustering.

Once you are ready, begin clustering using...

<Your Key word>

Once you have completed your cluster, continue to read.

Journal Exercise: Outline

Now that you have completed clustering your key word, try to produce as detailed and formal an outline as possible. With that in mind, here's what you do:

- Take a highlighter to your web of words and highlight any words and phrases (topics) that you think you should write about in your document.

- Jot down a major topic or section topic line, such as "benefits of outlines."

- Below your major topic, place the topic words or phrases in sequence (the order in which you think you will write about them) to produce a rough outline of your document.

- Expand your words and phrase to create full points.

- Add any additional related points and subtopic points. (In most instances, you will find them in your clustering. However, sometimes the act of moving from clustering to outline jogs your memory and helps you discover other points.)

- Review your draft outline and revise it as required based on your purpose, audience, and project scope; delete any irrelevant points; and fill in any other gaps between outline points with topics that come to mind as you review your outline.

Once you have completed your outline, continue to read.

If you are so inclined, you can try to write based on your outline. Treat each outline point and sub-point as the opening line of a directed freefall, and write from point to point. You don't have to write as quickly or subconsciously as you do when you freefall, but try to resist the urge to revise as you write. In other words, keep your writer separate from your editor.

If you are in the mood to read, however, carry on reading. There will be plenty of time for writing later, as we progress through the book.

6/ The Three Cs of Writing

In terms of content, before you write anything, you need to know, at minimum, your *W5—who, what, where, when* and *why*. We will look at the *W5* in greater detail later in the book. In addition, before you write, there are other *W*'s worth noting: *Who* are you and *who* is your reader? *What* you are writing about? *Why* you are writing? *What* do you want your reader to do, if anything?

The more you know before you write, the more likely you are to communicate all you have to write to achieve your purpose and motivate the action you desire. Also, the more you know before you write, the more likely you are to instinctively use the first three Cs of communication—clarity, conciseness, and coherence. You are also more likely to achieve the other two Cs: consistency and correctness.

Although you want to be as consistent and correct as possible when you write, consistency and correctness are more often achieved when editing a document. With that in mind, we will focus on the first three Cs in this chapter.

What exactly do the three Cs mean, and why are they important to business writing?

Conciseness, Clarity, Coherence

Conciseness means that you have removed extraneous words, phrases, clauses and sentences from your writing, without sacrificing important details or clarity. In other words, your writing emphasizes and supports the most important ideas in your document—those that help the reader understand your purpose and persuade the reader to take the action you need him or her to take.

Think of achieving conciseness as packing a single carry-on bag for a three-day business trip rather than encumbering yourself with a carry-on bag, suit bag, and suitcase—all containing articles of clothing and supplies you do not need and will not use.

Clarity is essential to understanding and is important if you are to achieve your purpose. If your readers do not understand what you want them to know or do, and if they do not understand why you want them to know or do it, then your document is not clear. If your writing is concise but not clear, you will not achieve your purpose.

To extend our packing imagery, think of packing one bag for your trip but reaching your destination only to realize that you forgot to pack your deodorant or some other vital accoutrement. You packed concisely, but not clearly.

Coherence means that the relationship between all the ideas presented in your document makes sense and supports your purpose and that your document reads in a unified, focused manner, progressing logically from point to point.

In terms of luggage, imagine if you were going to Montreal in the middle of winter and you packed winter socks and sandals instead of boots, or thick sweaters and shorts instead of pants. That is illogical—or incoherent—packing.

Writing that lacks conciseness, clarity, and coherence is ineffective and can lead to business problems—or worse. Poorly written business documents can cost an organization time and money, particularly if they lead to confusion and poor decisions. As for worse? Imagine that you are giving life-saving instructions and your writing is not concise, clear and coherent. Such writing can literally cost lives.

The backbone of clear, concise, coherent writing is planning and organization. If you invest time up front planning and getting organized, you will more likely employ the three Cs. In short, harness the writing process if you want to be an effective writer.

Or would you rather write like bureaucrats often write? Here's how a bureaucrat might write something:

We are less than pleased due to the fact that it is, at this point in time, the season of winter.

And here is how Shakespeare wrote it:

Now is the winter of our discontent.

I am not saying you have to write like Shakespeare to be effective; I am saying avoid writing in a bureaucratic manner to be effective.

When politicians deliver sentences like the one below, it may seem as if they are delivering a strong, effective statement.

First and foremost, we will ensure that each and every Canadian from coast to coast enjoys access to basic and fundamental health care. Finally and for good, we will put this serious health-care crisis behind us.

Frankly, if you were in a great hall and listening to a brilliant speaker, the above passage might sound inspirational. That's the art of speech writing: a speech needs to sound more dynamic than words on a page because it's spoken out loud. The above passage, however, falls flat on the page because it is not concise. Compare the above statement with the one below to see what I mean:

By ensuring that every Canadian has access to fundamental health care, we will put the health-care crisis behind us.

Let's look at another passage that could be more concise:

To write concisely, remove, delete, eliminate and eradicate extraneous, superfluous, redundant words, phrases, clauses and sentences—without sacrificing appropriate detail.

If you were to do what this passage says you should do, the revised passage would look something like this:

To write concisely, remove redundant words, phrases, clauses and sentences—without sacrificing appropriate detail.

On occasion, I've had people ask me if the edited passage should not look like this:

To write concisely, remove redundant words—without sacrificing appropriate detail.

You want to beware of writing so concisely that you end up sacrificing meaning. Words such as "remove," "delete," "eliminate" and "eradicate" are synonyms. You only need to use one of the words to make your meaning clear. The same can be said about "extraneous," "superfluous" and "redundant." On the other hand, "words," "phrases," "clauses" and "sentences" each mean something different. Cutting any of them would cut into the clarity of your meaning.

Applying the Three Cs

Let's apply what you've learned by editing a short passage and then editing an executive summary taken from an insurance industry white paper. (A white paper is a detailed report that proposes a solution to a major issue that a company, organization, or business sector is facing.) Make both samples as clear, concise and coherent as you can.

Here is the short passage. Read it and edit it, applying the three Cs:

Somebody has said that words are a whole lot like inflated money—the more of them that you use, the less each one of them is actually worth. Right on!

Go through the executive summary that can be found below this here passage just as many times as it takes to search out, find, and annihilate all the unnecessary and redundant words that you can find, as well as all the unnecessary and redundant phrases and sentences, and so on. Even delete and eliminate entire paragraphs, if required. But don't do it until after you have first and foremost completed an edit and revision of these here paragraphs!

Once you have edited the passage above, continue to read.

Note: At the end of this chapter, you will find edited versions of the above passage and of the executive summary below. Edit the above passage and the executive summary before you read the suggested revisions.

Executive Summary Exercise

The insurance industry executive summary is part of a formal document, so the tone should be formal; however, the writing should be free of clichés and buzzwords. The document is a tad technical and I want you to rewrite it for a business audience. In other words, it is your job to sort out the business issues the executive summary addresses and then improve the document for your primary audience—senior business executives—because they are the ones who must allocate funds. Before they will allocate funds and direct Information Technology (IT) staff to implement the solution proposed in this white paper, they must grasp the business issue and the need to resolve it.

Read the executive summary and edit it, applying the three Cs. You may want to read it several times and highlight the ideas and passages you want to keep. You can even go so far as to turn your highlighting into an outline that you will follow before you start to revise the passage.

In the face of amplified and increased competition and more intense rivalries, and in a climate of ongoing mergers and acquisitions and closer regulatory scrutiny than ever before, the life insurance industry is facing a myriad of operational, customer service, distribution channel and competitive pressures that can lead to the failure of companies.

The Information Technology (IT) departments in life insurance companies are expected to keep a really tight lid on spending while delivering innovative solutions that increase productivity, improve customer service, and open distribution channels.

At the same time, due to increases in mergers and acquisitions, most life insurance companies are running multiple IT administration systems that often do not communicate and interface with each other.

New replacement IT systems and IT conversion projects are often cost-prohibitive; however, multiple administration system environments are crippling the industry's ability to keep a lid on operational costs and keep expenses down, and they are impairing the opportunity to implement new customer service models that are so needed in today's increasingly competitive environment.

The end result of all of this is that IT departments are under greater and increasing pressure to preserve the investment in existing or legacy systems while somehow figuring out a way to provide customer-centric life insurance service delivery solutions. In addition, they need to deliver IT methods of allowing companies to work more productively, effectively, and efficiently with life insurance distributors who are dazed and confused by the myriad of IT administrative systems mixes out there.

Under such circumstance, what the heck is an unfortunate life insurance company to do?

Faced with these challenges, insurance companies need to adopt consolidation architecture. To put it as simply as possible, a consolidation architecture is a common, centralized interface that streamlines business processes through access to, and manipulation of, consolidated and standardized customer data across multiple administrative systems.

It's like having your cake and eating it too as a consolidation architecture preserves the existing legacy IT systems while facilitating their ability to communicate with each other. New programs developed for consumers or distributors (agents) can run on any system and be fully integrated.

Once you have edited the passage above, continue to read.

Revised Short Passage

Do not be concerned if your revised short passage is not exactly like the revised passage below. There is a degree of subjectivity to any writing.

Compare your revision to the one below and use it to help you determine if your revision is as clear, concise and coherent as it could be. Or, frankly, use your revision to determine if the one below is as clear, concise and coherent as it could be.

Someone once said that words are like inflated money—the more you use, the less each one is worth. Review the executive summary below and remove redundant words, phrases, sentences and even paragraphs if necessary. However, don't do it until you have edited this paragraph.

Revised Executive Summary

As with the paragraph revision exercise, do not be concerned if your revised executive summary is not like the revised passage below. Compare your revision to the one below to help you determine if your revision is as clear, concise and coherent as it could be.

In the face of increased competition, and in a climate of mergers and acquisitions and closer regulatory scrutiny, the life insurance industry faces numerous operational, customer service, and distribution channel pressures that need to be alleviated if companies are to succeed.

Life insurance Information Technology (IT) departments are expected to control spending while delivering solutions that increase productivity, improve customer service, and open channels to distributors (agents). However, due to mergers and acquisitions, most life insurance companies now run multiple IT administration systems that often do not communicate with each other, preventing IT staff from achieving these goals.

The ideal solution would be to replace existing IT systems with new ones. However, this is cost-prohibitive. Therefore, IT needs to preserve existing systems while providing solutions that enable life insurance companies to better serve customers and work more effectively with distributors.

Faced with these challenges, IT needs to adopt a cost-effective consolidation architecture—a centralized interface that allows multiple systems to communicate with each other.

With consolidation systems in place, IT can preserve legacy technology and streamline business processes across multiple systems. New business solutions, developed for consumers and distributors, can then be integrated with any system in the company.

To reiterate: your work does not have to look exactly like the work above to be effective. What you have to do, however, is eliminate the redundancies and write in as focused, clear and concise a manner as possible—while speaking to your target audience and achieving your purpose.

7/ Before Writing Articles

Before you write articles for newspapers, magazines, websites, corporate publications or any other periodical, there are a few things you should know. Ask any newspaper or magazine editor what they are looking for in a writer, a freelance writer for the sake of this list, and their Top ten list might look something like this:

- Develop great ideas appropriate to my audience
- Pitch me using clear, concise, focused query letters
- Follow up once, and then leave me alone
- Be open to negotiating the article's slant
- Conduct great research
- Conduct stellar interviews
- Deliver solid, focused, clean copy
- Meet your deadline
- Meet your word count
- Be open to discussing edits and revisions

Artistic creativity for articles in newspapers and magazines is limited, especially when compared to fiction or poetry magazines, as writing for periodicals tends to go through several phases:

- Story you propose (query letter for freelance writers)
- Story the editor negotiates with you
- Story you write and submit
- Story that comes out of the editing process

It is important to be able to work with your editor because there is a degree—sometimes a great degree—of collaboration required when writing for newspapers and, in particular, magazines. Magazine editors will often send your work back, asking for revisions or additional information.

At the same time, I've had many articles run with barely a word changed. Just don't go into the process expecting that. And, for what it's worth, contacts in the corporate market can be even more demanding—or picky—than periodical editors. Keep in mind: the editor is the gatekeeper between the reader and the publication, and the corporate client is the gatekeeper between the customers or internal staff (whoever you are writing for) and whatever document you are producing. They deserve to have a say, even a large one. Doesn't mean they will have a say, but it is their right to discuss anything you write with you.

If you are not flexible and open-minded—in other words, if you fall in love with your words—you may find yourself in conflict with editors or clients. You want to write the best darned document possible, but expect there to be editing. But this is not a book about editing, so let's figure out where to begin if you want to write the best darn news articles, profiles and feature articles possible.

Note: If you are interested in knowing more about the business of freelance writing for newspapers and magazines, consider picking up *Business of Freelance Writing: How to Develop Article Ideas and Sell Them to Newspapers and Magazines*. If you are interested in writing for corporate markets, consider *The Six-Figure Freelancer: How to Find, Price and Manage Corporate Writing Assignments*. And if you'd like to freelance for both markets, consider *Everything You Wanted to Know About Freelance Writing - Find, Price, Manage Corporate Writing Assignments & Develop Article Ideas and Sell Them to Newspapers and Magazines*. You can read more about all three books at www.paullima.com/books.

Read Before You Write

When Margaret Atwood was asked what advice she would give to any aspiring writer, she gave a one word answer: "Read." Atwood is a novelist and poet (although she has written non-fiction books and many articles). So I would suggest her advice is also true for aspiring non-fiction writers. Before you begin to write an article, you have to know your audience or reader. In other words, familiarize yourself with the tone, style and content of articles in the publication or website that you will be writing for.

As you read articles, ask yourself how the writing is influenced by the publication (business, consumer, lifestyle, political, industry-specific), the reader, the subject, the slant or angle, and the purpose of the article. Develop critical reading skills, become an analytical reader. Doing so will make you a better writer and, if you are a freelance writer, it will help you pitch query letters that are much more interesting and better targeted to the publication.

Pay particular attention to leads (also spelled "ledes")—the first paragraph, or first few paragraphs, of the article. Do the leads start with hard news, people, situations, settings, anecdotes, clichés, research results? Do they start in the past, present or future?

By reading and analyzing the leads (and there may be different styles of leads in one publication), you will discover how editors like their writers to start various types of articles. When writing articles for publications, you should mimic the leads of similar articles in the publication. With that in mind, two of the most important questions you can ask before you write are:

- Why do people read?
- Who are the readers of (publication X)?

Primarily, most people read because they want to be entertained or informed. Entertaining writing can be informative and informative writing can be entertaining. Whether you are writing to inform or to entertain depends to a large degree on:

- Type of publication
- Subject matter (topic) of article
- Slant (angle) you are taking on the subject
- Primary purpose of the article: inform, educate, entertain, teach, warn, solve, persuade, and so on.

Readers Are Not Homogeneous

Readers are not a homogeneous mass. They come in a variety of shapes, sizes, genders, colors, abilities and ages. They have a variety of needs and a variety of opinions. Readers of a particular magazine or newspaper, however, frequently share common demographics, political or religious beliefs, social attitudes, interests, concerns or hobbies. How can you tell what their similarities are? By what they read.

Do you read *Snowboarding Magazine*? If you do, you probably snowboard—just like the thousands of others who read it. And if you read it, you are probably (not necessarily, but most likely) male, 18 to 35, university-educated, with an above-average income. Suddenly the readers of *Snowboarding* start to look like a homogeneous mass—particularly to those companies that advertise in the magazine.

If you can prove to the editor of *Snowboarding* that you can meet the expectations of the readers—write in the tone and style (the language or lingo) of the readers—then you will enhance your chances of writing for the magazine.

So what are you going to write about and how are you going to meet readers' expectations? You determine what their interests and expectations are by reading the publication and looking at the advertisements. That determination will help you tailor your article pitch or query letter. (Much more on query letters in *Everything You Wanted to Know about Freelance Writing* – www.paullima.com/books.)

Journal Exercise: Analytical Reading

Westside Story. Love Story. Both works are modelled on Shakespeare's *Romeo and Juliet*, which was modelled on an older Italian play. What does that have to do with writing articles? Quite a bit if you are learning how to write articles.

As Margaret Atwood said when asked if she has any advice for neophyte writers, "Read." By this she means you should read analytically. So, before moving onto the next chapter, that's just what I want you to do.

Select news article and feature articles from newspapers, magazines or websites and do some analytical reading. Use your writer's journal to make notes.

You should read each article at least three times. Read it the first time for interest or pleasure. Read it the second time for understanding. After reading it the second time, write a synopsis of the article. Keep your synopsis to about seventy-five words.

As you read it the third time, answer the following questions:

- What type of article is it? A personal essay, opinion piece, editorial, hard news (current story), backgrounder to the news, a profile, how-to, in-depth analysis, investigative feature, something else?
- What is the subject matter or topic?
- What is the focus/slant/angle? (The writer's take on the topic.)
- What is the purpose of the article? Are you learning how to do something? Are you gathering useful information? Are you being entertained? Are you laughing or crying?
- Did you enjoy the writing? If so, what made it enjoyable? If not, why not?
- Was there conflict? If so, what is the main issue in conflict? Who is on what side of the issue? Is the issue resolved? If so, how? If not, why not?
- What captures your attention and what holds your interest—the conflict, the overall writing style or tone, the purpose, or all of the above?

Also, examine the writing structure of each article you analyze:

- How does the article start (the lead)?

- What does the writer do in the lead to draw you in? (The lead is generally the first paragraph or two of news articles; feature article leads are usually longer; more on leads later in the book.)

- If you were successfully drawn in, exactly how was it accomplished? What captured your attention?

- How does the writer keep you moving through the article? How does the writer keep you interested?

- How does the article end? Is it a satisfactory ending? Why or why not?

- Where in time and space does the story begin? Where does it end?

- How does the ending relate to the beginning, if at all?

- If the writer uses quotes or paraphrases, when, where and why does he do this?

This analytical reading exercise should be done a couple of times a week as you make your way through this book. You will learn a great deal about how to write and structure articles and the other documents we focus on in this book by reading analytically. If this feels like work, that's good. It is work—work that will make you a better writer. Analytical reading will make you a stronger, more informed, more polished writer—one who is more likely to get published.

And if you are so inclined and would like to do some writing before you move on, see if you can write an article that is structured in a similar manner to something you've just read. There will be plenty of time for writing as you work your way through this book, but if you feel like doing some article writing off the top, modelling something you've read is a good way to get started.

The goal is not to plagiarize something that has been previously written. Your goal is to learn from it and to apply what you learn to your own writing. Give it a shot, see where you go and what you learn.

8/ Overview: Types of Articles

We're going to look at an overview of news and feature articles here, followed by how to write leads for both, and then how to write full articles.

News Stories

News stories are often written in what is known as inverted pyramid style. Draw a one-dimensional pyramid (okay, a triangle). Now draw one upside down. Upside down, the "top" is much wider than the bottom. In a news article, the writer packs as much pertinent information into the first few sentences—the lead—usually answering the story's *W5* questions: *who, what, where, when* and *why*. The lead also sometimes answers *"how."*

News stories present the facts with little, or limited, embellishment. The paragraphs are short—sometimes only one or two sentences. The stories do not build to a climax or end with a grand flourish. Old-style news editors feel they should be able to cut off a news story anywhere after about the third paragraph (if not sooner) and run it. If you consider yourself a creative writer, that might make you say, "Ouch!" However, newspapers are often tight for space—it's those darn ads—and editors have to edit quickly.

I mentioned old-style news editors, but the fact is news stories have evolved. Once you get off the front page of the first section or the business section, you will find articles that read like magazine features. They are more story-like, with a beginning, middle and end.

Ironically, as newspapers include more features, many magazines are moving to shorter news and service (how-to or information-specific) articles. So, it helps if you are able to master both news and feature styles. (In addition to what you read in this book, I suggest you analytically read various types of articles to help you discern how to write them.)

Feature Articles

Just as newspapers used to be the primary domain of news stories, magazines were once the primary domain of feature articles. As mentioned, almost all major newspapers now run feature articles and traditional news stories. And most magazines run feature articles as well as short, breezy, newsy articles. Some magazines (*Maclean's* and *Time*, for instance) are more like newspapers than traditional magazines and some sections of newspapers are more like magazines.

Rather than having a newsy *W5* lead, the feature-article lead is meant to spark readers' interest and draw them into a long, leisurely look at a subject, person or event. The lead may focus on a scenario, a person or a detailed retelling of an event. It may pose questions. It may be blunt. It may seem, at first blush, to be obscure. If you see yourself writing feature articles, you owe it to yourself to read features analytically: see how they start, what effect the leads have on you, how they pull you into (or fail to pull you into) the story.

Because feature articles examine subjects or topics in detail, they usually involve a great deal of background research and a number of interviews. They are structured to keep the reader interested, often juxtaposing apparently contradictory details that draw the reader through to the conclusion of the feature. Editors will often work with you on the structure of a feature article. And they will never just lop off the end.

Soft Articles

In between news and feature articles are "soft" articles. They are not hard news articles nor are they feature articles. In terms of style, they come closer to features than news article, for the most part. However, some soft articles are written in news style. That is one reason you should read analytically before you write for a publication.

Soft articles can be found in newspapers and magazines and are generally short—two hundred to maybe nine hundred words. Typically, they focus on one topic (a new trend, how to do something, a personal or business profile, a preview or review, and so on). The articles may start with a *W5* lead, but the lead does not convey something that is breaking news. The articles may also start with non-news leads or feature-style leads that are shorter than long feature leads.

With all that in mind, we will look at these leads for all of these types of articles, and how to write them.

9/ Writing Article Leads

Why is the lead important? If you don't capture your reader's attention in the lead, chances are your article will remain unread. Freelance writers must capture the editor's attention in the lead of a query letter (the letter or email used to pitch a story idea) or chances are the article idea will not be read, let alone accepted. In addition, if you produce strong, dynamic leads, you will write in a more structured manner.

Many writers bury their leads. They try to build suspense—as one might with the opening of a novel. What you want to do, in fact, is set the stage for the article in your lead. I am not saying there cannot be suspense, but you have to build suspense sparingly and appropriately, generally in features. You would not try to build suspense in a hard-news lead or for a breaking-news story. If your lead is cute or witty but does not set the stage, establish important themes, and/or introduce significant characters or issues, it will fail.

Only the Beginning

Some editors will tell you that you have one or two paragraphs to capture the reader's attention. Some will tell you that you have one sentence. If the first sentence doesn't capture the reader's attention, the reader will not read on. Mind you, if the first sentence works, but the second doesn't, the reader may not continue reading so, as important as the lead is, what comes after it is vital too.

Having said that, the importance of the lead is sometimes—not always, but sometimes—exaggerated. I have read many articles from start to finish that have had dull leads. I have even read poorly written articles. Most of us have because the publication, type of article, subject matter, and/or the purpose of the article resonated with us or fulfilled a need. That doesn't mean you should try to get away with dull, poorly written leads. It just means some articles are read even if the leads are nothing special.

Let's take a closer look at the factors that affect your lead (and, in fact, the entire article):

Publication: Is it staid, conservative, liberal, sensational, radical, flip, satirical, commercial, non-profit, local, national or regional? Is it a newspaper, magazine, newsletter or annual report?

Subject matter: The topic you are writing about.

Type of article: Investigative, news, profile, column, obituary, filler, how-to...

Purpose of article: To inform, entertain, warn, solve problems, create controversy ...

Reader: Readers are not a homogeneous mass. They have a wide variety of needs and a wide variety of opinions. They read primarily because they want to be informed or entertained. Even then, they are not always consistent. Many readers want information presented in an entertaining manner. Others want it presented in a no-nonsense manner. A lot of what the reader expects depends on the overall tone and style of the publication they are reading.

What's entertaining to one reader may be dull to another. What's no-nonsense to one is a complex quagmire to another. Still, readers often share common values or interests. People who want information on computer monitors would probably pick up a copy of a computer publication if, on the cover, were the words: "Special Computer Monitor Issue." And they would likely read an article that started:

There are many different types of monitors you can buy for your computer. What you buy depends on what you want to do on your computer, and on what type of computer you have.

A pedestrian lead? Yes, but if the subject matter is of interest to me I'll read on, looking for information that is of value. Now, before editors kick me, allow me to say that I am not advocating dull, pedestrian leads that make readers snore. I am saying leads should be written in context and context includes the publication, subject matter, purpose of the article and the target readers.

The monitor article could have started:

Have you ever wanted to be Alice, absorbed into mystical colors as you fall through the looking glass? Colors so magical they could only be embraced in dreams—if you dream in rainbow-induced Technicolor. Well, this world, or as close as you will come to it without the use of hallucinogenic drugs, is yours to capture—if you have the right computer monitor.

As a reader, I might enjoy that lead, but if I have no interest in buying a computer monitor, I probably would not have read any farther. Conversely, I might find that lead pretentious but continue to read because I want to know more about computer monitors.

The writer may have had more fun creating the *Alice* lead, but is it appropriate? If I were the editor, I'd embellish the bland lead and tone down the over-written one. Does it seem subjective? In many ways, it is. But there are hard rules for lead writing too. Let's try to demystify leads by looking at what you should and should not do.

Leads in Greater Detail

How many words should your lead be? As long as necessary to draw your reader in and make a point. In short, there is no ideal number. Ten words may be appropriate under some circumstances, but one hundred words may work in other circumstances. Some feature articles have leads that are longer than many news stories. Whatever its length, the lead should leave the reader feeling as if something important awaits, that it will be worth his or her while to read on.

When writing leads, avoid clichés, generalizations, stereotypes, information overload, or any combination of the above, such as:

It's every parent's worst nightmare. Your child is playing outside and you hear the screech of brakes in front of your house followed by a thump.

Many stories start with "It's every parent's worst nightmare" and many of them focus on a silly or mundane topic. If it is truly a nightmare topic, don't tell me. Show me. Let your writing paint a nightmare picture. And if it not a nightmare situation, don't go there.

'Tis the season to be jolly. Ask the man with the white beard, red hat, and that special sparkle in his eye.

While there is technically nothing wrong with the above lead, it is overused during the Christmas season because it is easy to write. I suggest you put more effort into your writing, especially your lead, instead of leaning on something that has been used *ad nauseum*.

Nine out of ten doctors in Canada feel socialized medicine is on the road to ruin, but nine out of ten Canadians, while expressing some doubts about the effectiveness of the system, prefer it to the free enterprise, American model that leaves many people without adequate medical protection, which is why most Americans, especially those in middle class and lower income brackets, are interested in the Canadian health care system, even though the majority are leery of socialized medicine.

What do the doctors feel? Is it in sync with what Canadians feel? And what are Americans interested in? Furthermore, what do you think this article is really about? You should be enlightened by the lead, not confused by it.

In summary, your lead should focus on the subject matter and convey that focus in a clear and original manner. It should be clear, focused, creative and original. Read newspaper and magazine article leads on various topics. Try to model the leads you like in your writing. You can find numerous magazines and newspapers online (the list is way too long to compile; Google is your friend).

Lead Types

There are three basic types of leads: news lead (*W5* or hard lead), the non-news lead (soft lead), and the feature lead (soft lead generally used for, but not restricted to, long magazine articles). Within each category are a number of sub-categories.

The type of publication you are writing for, and the type of article you are writing, will influence your lead. For instance, you could be writing a news story, feature article, column, editorial, how-to article, and so on. We will focus on leads for news stories in this chapter, but will present a bit of information on non-news or soft leads. In the next chapter, we will look at soft and feature leads.

News leads include the *W5—who, what, where, when* and *why* (and sometimes *how*). There are several types of news leads, including the blind lead, summary lead, wrap lead and shirttail lead, which we will look at.

No matter what kind of news lead you are writing, you need to know your *W5*. That will help you determine the focus of your article and help you write your lead. The *W5* is so important, you should jot it down before writing. Even if you do not use a *W5* lead, you will need to cover those elements in your article, so make sure you know *who, what, where, when* and *why* (and *how*) before you start to write anything. With that in mind, let's look at some samples.

Sample W5 Leads

Here is a news headline followed by a W5 news lead:

Headline: Wildfire towns declared crime scenes

Lead: Police in Whittlesea, Australia declared incinerated towns crime scenes today, and the prime minister spoke of "mass murder" after investigators said arsonists may have set some of Australia's worst wildfires in history. The death toll rose to 166.

Deconstructing the W5, we see the following:

Who: police; the prime minister

What: declared incinerated towns crime scenes … spoke of "mass murder"

Where: Whittlesea, Australia

When: today

Why: investigators said arsonists may have set some of Australia's worst wildfires…

Here is another news lead followed by a breakdown of the W5:

Lead: Russians held impromptu memorial services on Tuesday at two subway stations in Moscow where suicide bombers conducted brazen attacks a day earlier that killed 39 people and stirred fears of a revival of terrorism here.

Here is the W5 outline:

Who? Russians

What? Held impromptu memorial services; killed 39 people and stirred fears of a revival of terrorism here

Where? At two subway stations in Moscow

When? On Tuesday; brazen attacks a day earlier

Why? Suicide bombers conducted brazen attacks … a revival of terrorism

Here is another news lead followed by a breakdown of the W5:

Lead: International Business Machines chairman and chief executive Louis Gerstner will face a friendlier group of shareholders at the annual meeting in Toronto today, after the computer giant last week posted surprisingly strong earnings for the last quarter.

Who? International Business Machines chairman and chief executive Louis Gerstner

What? will face a friendlier group of shareholders

Where? at the annual meeting in Toronto

When? today

Why? after the computer giant last week posted surprisingly strong earnings for the last quarter

Of course, the full articles expand on the *W5* and quote various sources; however, once you have the *W5*, you have the foundation of the story. And sometimes, once you have the *W5*, you have the entire story (as you will see in the "more American teenagers" lead in feature leads chapter). So the *W5* can be the foundation of anything you write and, at times, your *W5* can be all you need to write.

There are times journalists find multiple *W5* elements, or need more than the basic *W5* points, before they can write stories. There are times when they do not use all the *W5* points they find. Either way, *W5* is the place to start. I am suggesting that *W5* is the foundation of all writing. You should, in fact, know your *W5* before you start to write any non-fiction—news article for sure, but even longer features or short tweets. Again, it doesn't mean you will always use every W element, but know what they are before you write and make using them, or not, a conscious decision.

Let's look at some other W leads.

Sample W4 News Lead

You don't always have to use every W in your lead. However, you should be conscious of why you use the ones you use and why you leave out any of them.

Headline: Home prices to tumble in '09

Sub-head: Average decline to be nine percent

Lead: House prices are expected to fall eight percent across Canada this year and sales are predicted to slip nearly 17 percent, according to a new report from The Canadian Real Estate Association.

Deconstructing the W4, we see:

Who: Canadian Real Estate Association

What: house prices expected to fall eight percent

Where: across Canada

When: this year

Why: there was no reference to the economic downturn; however, with the spate of articles on the recession, including others on the same page, the why is apparent, so it was left out of the lead.

Summary Lead

Summary leads summarize the most important idea in the story. It is often preferred for breaking-news and issue-oriented stories. Here is a sample summary lead that contains little more than the *who* and *what*:

Lead: The University of Oregon must move more women into higher-level faculty jobs or face federal sanctions.

Blind Lead

A blind lead is a summary lead that leaves out potentially confusing detail(s), as in this example:

Lead: The state's land-use planning agency on Friday chose a former city planner from New York to be its new director.

This lead omits the name of the planning agency (the Department of Land Conservation and Development) and the name of the city planner, who was relatively unknown. A catch-all paragraph (or nut 'graph—the story in a nutshell) immediately follows a blind lead and would include specific details omitted from the lead.

Wrap Lead

To "wrap" a lead, you combine, refer to or wrap several items in a lead.

Lead: Thursday's storm caused the deaths of a Hamilton woman who broke her neck in a fall, a Niagara Falls man who had a heart attack while shovelling snow and a Fort Erie teenager struck by a skidding car.

Shirttail Lead

Shirttails include a summary lead focusing on the most newsworthy elements, followed by the remaining items (or shirttails), each with its own lead. Shirttails are often used for meeting stories. The first lead targets the most important item on the agenda; remaining items are introduced with an "in-other-business" transition in the second paragraph.

Lead: A man taking photographs of Portland's skyline about 2:15 a.m. Sunday was struck by a car and knocked into the Willamette River off the Interstate 5 ramp to Interstate 84. Another accident later that morning, this one involving a hit-and-run driver in Southwest Washington, left a Lynnwood, Wash., man in serious condition.

Complex Shirttail Lead

Similar to the Shirttail lead, the Complex Shirttail lead includes a summary lead focusing on the most newsworthy elements. But that lead is followed by a number of related elements.

Lead: The federal government has provided nearly $400 million for desperately needed affordable housing in Ontario—but the money may not be spent any time soon.

The province has stashed the money in a contingency fund pending the outcome of a fiscal battle with Ottawa.

Now, housing groups are wondering whether the province will ever spend the money on housing.

Notice the multiple *who*'s and related *what*'s in the above lead. Each source has equal weight. Each who is given its own paragraph and its own what to make it clear there are three sides to the story; the conflict makes this topic newsworthy.

Deconstructing the who and what from the above lead we find:

Who: federal government

What: provided nearly $400 million for desperately needed affordable housing

Who: The province

What: has stashed the money in a contingency fund

Who: housing groups

What: are wondering whether the province will ever spend the money on housing

You should be able to find the multiple where's, when's and why's in the lead as well.

W5 Lead from Corporate Article

W5 leads are not just used in news articles in newspapers and magazines. The lead (and second paragraph) below was taken from the website of Statistics Canada, a government agency. This article is presented as news as it is reporting on the release of a new statistic.

Article: The top 1% of Canada's 25.5 million tax filers accounted for 10.6% of the nation's total income in 2010, down from a peak of 12.1% in 2006.

In the early 1980s, the top 1% of tax filers held 7.0% of the total income reported by all tax filers. This proportion edged up to 8.0% in the early 1990s and reached 11.0% by the early 2000s.

Who: The top 1% of Canada's 25.5 million tax filers

What: accounted for 10.6% of the nation's total income; down from a peak of 12.1% in 2006

Where: Canada

When: 2010

Notice that the why is not there; it could be argued that it is not the agency's responsibility to speculate as to why the change occurred. That is best left up to politicians, commentators and news outlets. But the primary point to pick up on here is that this W style of lead writing is not the exclusive domain of news articles that appear in newspapers and magazines. It is a style that appears in periodical and business writing because it conveys the most pertinent information—the information that readers want. That does not mean you can't have an article that, in the above instance, focuses on the why or takes an editorial stance. But you, the writer, need to know what you are writing about and the publication you are writing for—the kind of person who will be reading the article and what are they primarily interested in.

W5 Lead from One-Source Article

Here is a sample W5 lead from a one-source article:

Lead: Ontario's economy is in for a slowdown, says Canada's central banker, as the U.S. housing and auto sectors cool, spilling across the border.

Although Ontario's economy will continue to grow in the next 12 months, it will probably turn in the worst performance among the provinces, Bank of Canada governor David Dodge said today.

Deconstructing the W5, we see:

Who: Ontario's economy

What: is in for a slowdown; turn in the worst performance among the provinces

Where: Ontario; in Canada

When: the next 12 months

Why: the U.S. housing and auto sectors cool, spilling across the border

Paraphrasing and Quoting

Notice how the writer yields to a higher authority by using two paraphrases in the above lead. In other words, the writer does not quote Dodge in the lead; he does, however, refer to Dodge. Why reference Dodge in the lead? Dodge is the governor of the Bank of Canada. If Paul Lima says something about the economy, it's not news and it would not be reported. If the governor of the Bank of Canada says it today, it is news and it must be attributed to him.

Dodge is the only source in this article. He gave a speech on the economy today. That's news. Reporters can get comments from bankers, economists, and others for follow-up articles that they can write for tomorrow's edition of the newspaper.

But why paraphrase, not quote Dodge? Often, the gist of a comment is all you need to set the stage for the article. To quote Dodge in the lead would require too many words to say the same thing. By paraphrasing, the reporter establishes that comments by Dodge will be the focus of the article. The lead covers the *W5* and establishes Dodge as the central figure, and then the writer quotes him several paragraphs in:

"It is important to think of this as a mild and likely short-lived, cyclical slowdown," Dodge said in a speech televised to the Ontario Economic Leadership Summit in Niagara-on-the-Lake.

Eight paragraphs into a twelve-paragraph article, the reporter presents another side of the story, again paraphrasing Dodge:

Dodge conceded those forecasts could be off, however, if consumers decide to start spending even more. And they might.

Putting this information right after the lead would have undercut the news. Mind you, you might call not putting it in right after the lead "sensationalizing the news," and you might be right.

However, newspapers tend to present the "sexy" side of the story first, and then fill in with additional facts that give a story balance and make it seem objective.

Again, in this article, the reporter does not quote anyone else. This article focused on the speech the day after it was given. The business sections of newspapers can do a more in-depth analysis tomorrow, and quote other sources. In other words, the theme of this story has legs—it will run for several days.

What about How?

Read more news stories; focus on the lead to see how the writer has worked the most pertinent *W5* details into it. Then see how those details play out through the rest of the story. Look for conflict and consensus—people on opposite sides of issues butting heads in the article or people in agreement.

One thing you might notice as you do your reading is that *how* is seldom used in the lead. As one reporter friend of mine points out, "Sadly, it's most often neglected by journalists who just don't think to ask, 'Just how did this happen?' or 'Just how is this supposed to work?'" Keep your eyes open, though, and see if you can find how in any leads. If you find one, ask why it was used. And when you don't find it, ask yourself why it was not used and if it should have been included.

Use Active Voice

When writing leads, use active voice (who did what to whom), not passive voice (what was done to whom by whom). Active voice uses fewer words and engages the reader more than passive voice does. Let's look at active voice in the first *W5* lead presented in this chapter, and then convert it to the passive voice so you can see the difference.

Active: Police in Whittlesea, Australia declared incinerated towns crime scenes today.

Passive: Incinerated towns were declared crime scenes today by police in Whittlesea.

Active: Fire destroyed a house on Main Street early Monday morning.

Passive: A house was destroyed by fire on Main Street early Monday morning.

Journal Exercise

Now it's your turn to write a couple of news leads. I'll give you a couple of *W5*s that you can convert into leads. So that you have some background on each story, I am going to give you *more information* than you would jot down before writing an article. Don't feel you have to use every word in the *W5*s in your leads.

I also encourage you to find your own *W5*s and convert them into leads. Have a bit of fun with it. What are you or friends or members of your family up to? Turn a particular activity into a *W5* lead. Is there anything new or different going on at work or school? *W5* it. And, of course, if you have to write anything in particular for work or school, ask yourself if a *W5* lead would be appropriate. If so, outline your *W5* and then write your lead.

Who: Rob Ford, mayor of Toronto; three-judge Divisional Court panel

What: panel overturned guilty verdict of conflict of interest charge (for voting on a city council request that he pay back money improperly solicited for his football team charity using city hall letterhead); Ford remains mayor of Toronto

Where: Toronto, Ontario

When: January 25, 2013

Why: appeal panel accepted Ford's argument that council didn't have the authority to order him to pay back the $3,150; Ford's vote, the panel agreed, was null and void

Who: Boy Scouts of America

What: eliminated ban on gays as serving as scout leaders; ban was reaffirmed in Scout policy seven months ago; local chapters will be able to decide whether to admit gay scouts

Where: America; local chapters

When: January 28

Why: acknowledged that scouting, like a multicultural and sexually diverse modern America, could no longer impose such a policy from headquarters

Write at least three W5 leads before you read on.

Applying W5 to Email

Although this is not a general business writing book, I want to show you how you can short cut the writing process by using the *W5* and applying it to a simple email message. Answering the *W5* questions allows you to think about these points:

- Your audience (*who*)
- Your purpose (*why*)
- Your topic or subject (*what*)
- Any action the reader should take (what, w*hen*, *where* and perhaps *how*, the sixth W)

Although it's called the *W5*, answering the sixth W, how, can help you determine if you need to give the reader explicit instructions concerning any action you require.

Once you've answered the W5 questions, you can take these steps:

- Review your answers and decide what you will include and what you will exclude when writing your message.
- Arrange your points in the order in which you should address them—your formal outline.
- Write from point to point.
- Revise as may be required.
- Hit send.

In short, answering *W5* questions lets you prepare, conduct internal research and organize your thoughts before you write.

10/ Full News Articles

As you move from the *W5* lead into the full news article, you should connect the W dots, so to speak, for the reader. In other words, you should expand on the most important Ws, as you will see in this weather-related story. (**Note:** "GTA" in the article below stands for Greater Toronto Area; readers of the Toronto Star would know this). First, let's look at the *W5*:

Who: commuters

What: are enduring a tough morning in the GTA

Where: in the GTA

When: Monday

Why: a low-pressure system brought heavy snow to the streets

Now let's look at the full article:

Monday commuters are enduring a tough morning in the GTA after a low-pressure system brought heavy snow to the streets.

School buses have been cancelled in York, Peel Halton and regions outside the GTA.

Freezing rain started around 7:30 a.m. but the precipitation is much lighter than the early morning snowfall. Environment Canada says rain is expected this afternoon, followed by high temperatures this week.

Heavy snow across the GTA has caused numerous collisions on the main highways, including a tractor-trailer that jackknifed on the eastbound QEW in Burlington near Brant St. None have led to serious injuries.

School buses are cancelled for both public and Catholic schools in the following regions: York, Peel (including Dufferin-Peel), Halton. Durham north of Hwy. 7 (Brock, Uxbridge and Scugog), Waterloo, Wellington-Dufferin (including Guelph).

Schools are still open and many secondary-school exams have been delayed.

Air Canada, Porter Airlines and WestJet are all warning of possible delays and advising travellers to check their flight status.

Environment Canada expects four centimetres of snow to accumulate before temperatures drop this afternoon, changing freezing rain to normal showers.

A warm front is expected to arrive from Colorado early Tuesday, with a forecasted high of 8C and a possible record-breaking 12C Wednesday.

Would it be fair to say that every aspect expands on some component of the lead? The "school buses" of the second paragraph are "commuters" and they have been cancelled in various areas inside and outside the GTA. The "freezing rain" fell below the heavy snow, starting "around 7:30 a.m." on Monday. "Environment Canada" (a weather agency) is not quoted, but information from the agency is provided. Yes, it looks beyond "Monday" but think of your reader: they'd want to know how long this issue will last.

Of course the "heavy snow" (check out our "why") "across the GTA" (where) "has caused numerous collisions on the main highways" (would that not involve our "*who*?"). You can go on and apply this analysis to the full article. Key is that all the elements are related to and build on the *W5*.

Let's look at another news article, this one from the *New York Times*. But first the *W5*. Notice the missing elements:

Who: Toyota Motor
What: sold a record 9.75 million vehicles
Where: global sales – not mentioned in the article but look at the headline
When: last year

We don't see the "why" until nine paragraphs in: "production rebounded and the automaker went on an offensive to win back market share." The article is not about why Toyota is number one, but that Toyota is number one. Other articles will spell out in detail why Toyota has bounced back. But that is not the *focus* of this particular article. The news is that Toyota has bounced back. Follow up articles can *focus* on why this has occurred.

That is something you must ask yourself (or your editor) before you write: What is my focus? I could not imagine writing an article without knowing that small, yet major, bit of information.

With all that in mind, here is the full article:

Headline: Toyota Returns to No. 1 in Global Auto Sales

Article: Toyota Motor sold a record 9.75 million vehicles last year, according to an official tally released Monday, roaring past General Motors and Volkswagen to reclaim its title as the world's top automaker in 2012.

General Motors, which held the top spot in 2011, mustered 9.29 million vehicles in global sales last year. The U.S. company had been the top-selling automaker for decades before losing its lead to Toyota in 2008. Volkswagen sold 9.1 million vehicles last year, a record for the German automaker, which has expanded its presence in emerging markets. VW also outsold Toyota in 2011.

Toyota estimated last month that it sold 9.7 million vehicles for the year, and final figures released Monday were slightly higher.

By confirming its No. 1 title, Toyota cements a strong comeback from several years of tumbles.

A sharp slowdown in exports during the global economic crisis led to the automaker's biggest loss in decades, while controversy over its handling of recalls greatly tarnished its image for quality and reliability.

In 2011, the earthquake and tsunami in Japan, as well as widespread flooding in Thailand later that year, severely disrupted production, weighing on sales in important markets like the United States and pushing Toyota to No. 3 in global sales.

Toyota had a bumper year in 2012, however, as production rebounded and the automaker went on an offensive to win back market share. Toyota sales in the United States surged 27 percent, to 2.08 million vehicles. In Japan, sales rose 35 percent, to 2.41 million units, helped by government incentives for fuel-efficient cars.

Those increases were enough to offset a decline in sales in China, where Japanese businesses have been hurt by consumer boycotts amid a bitter territorial dispute between the two countries. In Europe, sales of Toyota cars rose by 2 percent. Toyota's sales figures include deliveries from its subsidiaries Hino Motors and Daihatsu Motor.

The other automakers among Japan's big three also sold more cars in 2012 and are set for even higher sales this year on the back of a weaker yen, which makes Japanese-made cars and parts more price competitive. Honda Motor said global sales jumped 19 percent to 3.82 million vehicles, while Nissan Motor logged a 5.8 percent sales growth to 4.94 million vehicles.

This year, Toyota aims to improve on its record for this year to sell 9.91 million cars worldwide.

Notice how the article looks at more than Toyota. It looks at General Motors and Volkswagen—where they were in relation to Toyota and where they are now. Although the focus is not on the rebound, the article does look at where Toyota was as opposed to where it is now. That context helps make this exciting news (if you are interested in the automotive industry) as opposed to ho-hum news, "Toyota is still on top." And, of course, because this is a US publication, the article looks at specific sales figure in the US. But it doesn't just look at the US as this is about (is focused on) global sales, so it looks at what's happening in China and Europe as well.

Let's look at a final news article, this one from *Maclean's* a Canadian news magazine. But first, the headline and the *W5*. Notice, when you get to the article, that you will not find the why upfront. It shows up from two perspectives, Japan's and Canada's, later in the article.

Headline: Japan relaxes imported beef restrictions for 4 countries including Canada

Who: Japan

What: is relaxing restrictions on imported beef from four countries including Canada

Where: Japan, four countries

When: Feb. 1; a decade after raising barriers amid the so-called mad cow disease scare

Why: following public hearings (third paragraph); efforts are getting results (sixth paragraph)

Now the full article, with some commentary in [square brackets] in the article. Notice who gets quoted and where the quotes are placed. This article is all about Japan lifting restrictions but the article quotes a couple of Canadians. *Maclean's* is a Canadian news magazine, so the readers would be more interested in Canada's reaction to this news, than they would be in anything Japanese spokespeople had to say about the why. But before we get to the reaction, we have to present the news so that we, the readers, know what the Canadians are reacting to.

Article: Japan is relaxing restrictions on imported beef from four countries including Canada, a decade after raising barriers amid the so-called mad cow disease scare. [Canada is the only country named as this is running in a Canadian news magazine.]

Japan's Foreign Ministry announced Monday that it will allow imports of beef from cows up to 30 months old, effective Feb. 1. The previous standard was to ban imports of beef from animals older than 20 months. [This sentence elaborates on the restriction relaxing mentioned in the lead.]

The Canadian government estimates the potential market value of beef exports to Japan will rise to between $140 million and $150 million a year, about double what they have been under the tighter rules. [This gives us the value implications of the regulation relaxing; notice this is the Canadian government estimate. Just because it's a Canadian news magazine doesn't mean everything will be from a Canadian perspective; it all depends, though, on the story and the focus the editor (representing the readers) wants.]

Japan's Health Ministry approved the step—which also applies to beef imports from the United States, France and Netherlands—following public hearings. [This sentence elaborates on the *who*, Japan, mentioned in the lead. Notice how the other countries are mentioned, now that we have some of the Canadian focus out of the way. This is not what you'd read in a US or British publication, which makes sense.]

Canada's government issued a statement from Ottawa welcoming the change in rules. "As part of our government's plan to create jobs, growth and long-term prosperity for all Canadians by opening new markets, we have been working closely with Japan to expand access for our exporters," said Trade Minister Ed Fast. [The quote could be from a Japanese spokesperson, elaborating on why this move was taken, but do Canadian readers care? They want to know the implications for Canada.]

"Today's announcement is proof that these efforts are getting results, and we look forward to taking our trading relationship with Japan to the next level through an Economic Partnership Agreement which would provide additional export opportunities for Canadian businesses."

The beef industry's marketing arm, Canada Beef Inc., said the decision could "potentially double Canadian beef sales to Japan. Japanese customers will soon enjoy increased availability of high-quality Canadian beef, and Canada's cattle producers and beef industry will greatly benefit from increased trade with Japan," the organization said in a release. [A second source, also Canadian, representing the beef industry, is quoted. The quote comes from a media release, but it could also come from an interview with the industry spokesperson.]

Japan banned beef imports in 2003 from several countries after a fatal brain disease was discovered in a few animals, leading to concern that eating their meat could pose a health risk for humans. [Why is this so far down, not closer to the top? The answer is simple: this is old news. It is relevant for those who don't know what was done or why, but this is not the current news. It's what is often referred to as "background" and it comes later in an article. If there was only room for five paragraphs in the magazine, the article could have been cut at paragraph five; the background would not be missed by most readers. This is the inverted pyramid style of writing news.]

Canadian beef producers were hit hard by the import bans imposed by Japan and other countries, including the United States. The Canadian monitoring system was also criticized and later improved.

In 2005, Japan allowed imports of beef 20 months or younger.

In summary, when writing news articles, outline your *W5* before you start to write. Sometimes you might have multiple *who*'s or *what*'s, and so on. Jot them all down. You will quickly see which *W*'s should be linked logically with which other Ws. Ask yourself what your focus is, or should be. This is generally related to the publication and the main readers of the publication. If in doubt, discuss it with your editor. But have a focus.

Use the inverted pyramid style of writing—the most important *W*'s up front, and elaborate on the most important *W*'s closer to the lead. Include quotes when and where appropriate, related to, and elaborating on, the most important Ws. Let the least important information, based on your *W*'s and focus, come last.

If the editor had to shorten the article, would the last paragraph be missed? The second last? The third last? If your answer is "yes," then you are burying important information and not using the inverted pyramid style. (Please see "more American teenagers" lead in the feature leads chapter.)

Journal Exercise

Now it's your turn to write a couple of news articles. For this exercise, feel free to turn any of the leads from the previous exercise into longer articles. To do so, you can interview a source or two or you can conduct a bit of online research. Find two or three sources that have written about the topics, take notes as you read what each source has produced (as if you were interviewing the source), and then create your own news article.

Focus on the news aspect, in other words avoid editorializing or expressing your own opinion on either topic. Start with a strong *W5* lead, transition into the article, looking at both (or all) sides of the issue, and include one or two quotes.

On the other hand, if you have something specific that you want to write about, or if you produced leads based on what you or friends or members of your family are up to, feel free to turn any of those leads into news articles.

Write one or two news articles, including a couple of quotes, before you read on.

11/ Soft Articles and Leads

As you may have gathered by now, rather than using the *W5* to deliver the news, soft leads and feature leads capture the attention of readers by using a story-related anecdote, painting a picture of a person, place or thing, or posing a question. The paragraph that follows a soft lead, which might go on for several paragraphs or more depending on the nature and length of the articles, is called a nut 'graph—the article in a nutshell—and often contains the most important *W5* elements.

Feature article leads draw the reader into a longer, more leisurely (sometimes contentious) look at a subject, person, event or situation. Feature leads are similar to soft leads but they tend to go into more detail and establish the major theme(s) and conflict(s) of the story. Often setting up opposing points of view, the feature lead might focus on a person, a detailed retelling of an event or a detailed recreation of a scene or setting.

Unlike news articles that often peter out toward the end (inverted pyramid), feature articles have defined beginnings (lead), middles (body), and ends (conclusion). The longer, more leisurely lead is a staple of feature writing for magazines, but they can be used in longer newspaper articles as well. The middle builds on the opening, putting flesh on the bones of the themes, characters, or conflicts introduced in the lead. And the end often concludes the article and reflects or echoes the beginning as well. In other words, readers often feel as if they have come full circle when they get to the end of a feature article.

Poster Child Lead: Why a W5 Lead Was Not Used

The article below could start with a *W5* news lead about the economic downturn. Instead, it starts with a three-paragraph human interest lead, known as a soft lead (rather than a hard news lead). There are many types of soft leads. This particular lead is called a poster child lead. The poster child is the one who represents the many.

Headline: "There aren't even jobs to bag groceries" in Calgary

Lead: Cassandra Lees has found herself in a situation she would have thought impossible just a year ago—unemployed and unable to find work anywhere in Calgary.

When Lees, 28, moved to the city three years ago from Winnipeg, she couldn't walk down the street without seeing a "Help Wanted" sign in every retail window. Employers were offering trips to new recruits and giving away cars as incentives to employees.

Now, after months of looking for everything from secretarial work to retail positions, Lees said she is painfully aware of a new reality. "There aren't even jobs out there to stock shelves or bag groceries," she said.

Nut 'graph: No province is immune to declining fortunes, but Alberta's fall, after such dramatic highs as last summer's oil and gas prices, is steeper than anywhere else. The province's economic activity is projected to fall by 2.3 percent this year, the sharpest drop among the provinces, according to an RBC report. Capital investments in the province have scaled back significantly, most noticeably in drilling for new wells.

Note: The full article, and several other articles, can be read in Appendix I at the end of the book.

The reason a soft lead, a poster child lead in this instance, was used is simple. This article was written part way through the economic downturn of 2008 and there had been many news articles on the downturn. In other words, the economic downturn was not news. The poster child lead—again, the one person who represents the many (in this case the many who had felt the toll of the downturn)—puts a human face on the issue. But notice how it still gets to the news in the fourth paragraph—the nut 'graph or the article in a nutshell.

In short, if a story plays out over days, weeks, months, or even years ("has legs," in journalism parlance) it often moves from a news story to a human interest story. It can become a news story again if there are new developments, as we saw with Japan altering its beef ban in the previous chapter. The human interest story still has to contain elements of the news (again, as you will see by the nut 'graph and some other background information) but the lead puts a human face on the story.

Additional Poster Child Lead

You don't want to bury breaking news under a soft lead; however, if the story is not a breaking news story (if it's a profile, a how-to article or even a follow-up to a news story, for example), start with an appropriate soft lead.

For instance, as I was writing the first draft of this chapter, there were a number of news stories about the economic downturn. Is it a recession? Will it become a depression? What caused it? How can we get out of it? Whenever you have a newsworthy trend—economic, political, legal, social, cultural, medical, technological, and so on—you will find interesting follow-up articles that explore niche aspects of the trend. They tend to use soft leads, as in the poster child example below.

Headline: In a shrinking workforce, women may surpass men

Lead: When Angie Dick heard her husband might be laid off at his factory job, she knew it was time to start working.

"I hadn't worked for 13 years after I was disabled in a car crash," said Angie, 44. In September, she started working as a sales representative for Kresslor Personnel, an employment agency in Mississauga.

Mark was laid off at his oil-drum refurbishing job two weeks ago.

In the next paragraph in the article, the nut 'graph, we find the news:

As the economic downturn gets worse, experts say Dick is part of a trend in which women find it easier to get jobs, and could soon outnumber men in the workforce as jobs in the manufacturing sector decline—an area traditionally dominated by men.

The last time women surpassed men in employment was World War II.

The soft lead is enticing because this is not a hard news story. It is a follow-up to hard news stories about the economic downturn. It relates directly to the economic downturn but details a by-product of the downturn and speaks to wider social implications of the downturn. Dick is, of course, our poster child representing the women who are getting jobs as traditional, male-oriented positions disappear.

Poster Child Lead and Quote Paragraphs

The poster child is the most often used soft lead or lead used in a longer feature article, so it is worth looking at another one.

Headline: Keeping an Eye on Bouncing Prices Online

Lead: Jen Hughes used to have the time to hunt for online coupon codes and refresh her web browser to see if the clothes she wanted had gone on sale yet. But after she had her first child, she said, trying to track e-commerce prices had to go.

Quote Paragraph: "I spend my day chasing my daughter around, so I don't have the luxury of sitting at my computer," said Ms. Hughes, 29, of Reading, Mass. Many sites "have sales every other day, but I don't have time to go on and see if the things I actually want have made it onto the sale yet."

Now she doesn't have to.

Nut 'graph: With retailers' Internet prices now changing more often—sometimes several times within the space of a day—a new group of tools is helping shoppers outwit the stores. Rather than requiring shoppers to do the work by entering an item into price-comparison engines throughout the day, the tools automatically scan for price changes and alert customers when the price drops.

Notice the W5 in the nut 'graph:

Who: retailers

What: Internet prices now changing more often; a new group of tools is helping shoppers outwit the stores

Where: Internet

When: within the space of a day

Why: Rather than requiring shoppers to do the work

The article goes on to examine some of the "new group of tools" that the nut 'graph talks about and how and why they are being used. In other words, the article does not build on Jen Hughs. It builds on what the article is all about—the tools. That does not mean you cannot write an article about Jen Hughs. It means that she is not the focus of this article. She is, however, the human interest lead who represents the many and who captures the attention of the reader and draws the reader into this article.

Body: Some tools, including one from Citibank's Citi Card, even scour sites for lower prices after a purchase and help customers get a refund for any price difference.

Websites that help shoppers compare prices and track online deals have existed as long as e-commerce itself. But rapid changes in pricing at many major retailers have made it more difficult for shoppers to keep on top of it all.

The research company Dynamite Data, which follows prices on behalf of retailers and brands, tracked hundreds of holiday products at major retailers in 2011 and 2012. During a two-week period around Thanksgiving, Amazon and Sears were changing prices on about a quarter of those products daily, a significant increase from the previous year. Walmart, Toys "R" Us, Kmart and Best Buy also changed prices more frequently in 2012.

Even the web browser a customer uses can make a difference. The website Digital Folio, which shows consumers price changes, did side-by-side comparisons of televisions. On Newegg using the Chrome browser, the firm was offered a $997 price on a Samsung television. Using Firefox and Internet Explorer, the price was $1,399.

The firm found a difference on another Samsung television model at Walmart.com, where using Firefox yielded a $199 price and Chrome and Internet Explorer $168.

Finally, we come to the more detailed second and third quote paragraphs.

Quote paragraphs are, as the name implies, paragraphs that include quotes based on interviews with your sources. In this article, the first quote paragraph quotes an expert who reinforces that price changes can have an effect on consumers. The second quote paragraph, after another paragraph that describes a new tool, gives us more detail on how the tool works and what effect it has on (see the previous quote) consumer behaviour.

Quote paragraph #2: "A lot of times the price will have a big difference on consumer behavior," said Larry S. Freed, chief executive of ForeSee, which analyzes customer experiences.

One of the new price-tracking tools is Hukkster, introduced last year by two former J. Crew merchants. It asks shoppers to install a "hukk it" button on their browsers. Then, when a shopper sees an item she likes, she clicks the button, chooses the color, size and discount she is interested in, tells Hukkster to alert her when the price drops, and waits for an email to that effect.

Quote paragraph #3: "We wanted a way to know, on a specific style we want, when it goes on sale," said a co-founder, Erica Bell. Hukkster also looks for coupon codes that apply to specific items, so a J. Crew nightshirt that was originally $128 came out to $62.99 after a site markdown combined with a 30 percent discount code that Hukkster found.

As you read this and other articles analytically, you will begin to see how well-written articles are tightly woven around a theme that is established in a news lead or a nut 'graph of a soft lead.

The rest of the article that tells us a bit more about how this works for the companies, or at least one of the companies, offering this service and then … Who is that we see in the article toward the end? Why Ms. Hughs. In soft articles, the poster child often comes back toward the end to bring the reader full circle. Notice how our poster child's name is used: she is "Ms. Hughs." She could be referred to as "Hughs" with no Ms., which is common in many publications. Others like to use the honorific (Mr. or Ms.) the second time they use the last name of anyone referred to or quoted in an article. Read analytically to see if publications your are writing for use the honorific or not. Follow whatever style they use.

Rest of the article: Currently, Hukkster makes money from referral traffic—it is paid a fee when shoppers buy something via a link from its emails. The founders say they are approaching retailers about ways of working with them by, for instance, offering personalized discounts based on shoppers' "hukks."

"Retailers are forced to do, say, 30 percent off all sweaters when what they're really trying to move is the green merino sweater. This provides them the option to do that on a one-to-one basis," a co-founder, Katie Finnegan, said.

Ms. Hughes, the Massachusetts mother, "hukks" items in specific sizes and colors, and then waits for the notification, like one on a Boden sweater she recently bought for her daughter.

"Now, of course, I'm hukking everything under the sun, including diapers, which I don't think is their target audience," she said.

Digital Folio charts the 30-day price history on electronics items at a number of retailers so shoppers can see not only where the lowest price is, but also whether that price might go lower still.

Additional Soft Leads

Below is another soft lead example. This one might feel like a poster child, but the celebrity used in the lead has not been interviewed for the article. As you will see, the lead uses events that are in the public domain to lead somewhere. Where? We'll find out when we get to the nut 'graph, of course.

> **Lead**: The campaign ad opens with a familiar boyish face, now atop a body that sways uncontrollably. Michael J. Fox, wearing a shirt and suit jacket, talks directly to the camera.
>
> "They say all politics is local, but it's not always the case," Fox says in the 30-second commercial backing Senate candidate Claire McCaskill in Missouri, a Democrat. "What you do in Missouri matters to millions of Americans—Americans like me."
>
> Fox, who suffers from Parkinson's disease and supports research on embryonic stem cell for a potential cure, also has lent his celebrity to Democrats Benjamin L. Cardin, running for the Senate in Maryland, and Wisconsin Gov. Jim Doyle, who is seeking re-election. Both politicians also back stem cell research.

Again, the news in the nut 'graph follows the soft lead, and the news is not about Fox being diagnosed with Parkinson's disease. That happened well before this article was written and had been fully covered. This article is about Fox and the backlash to his commercials. Here is the news:

> The ads, released today, have triggered a backlash, with some criticizing them as exploitive. Conservative radio commentator Rush Limbaugh has claimed Fox was "either off his medication or acting."

The soft lead is enticing because this is not a hard-news story, even though the ads were released "today." Had war broken out today, or had a bank been robbed, that would be hard news. This is soft news because it is a spat between celebrities, because Fox is famous and is ill, and because Limbaugh is a jerk. (Sorry, I could not help but editorialize!)

Situation Lead

Here is an attention-grabbing situation lead that any editor might like to see around Mother's Day or Valentine's Day: It uses people, but it is not a poster child lead. Although what is happening to the people is important, and there is a specific example, the situation (what is causing the issue) is more important.

Lead: The same bunch of roses that says "I love you" to a mother or "I'm sorry" to a lover could mean long-term illness in communities where they were grown. Doctors studying the issue in Ecuador have revealed the thorny side of the cut-rose industry as they work toward a fairer flower.

The predominantly young workers who toil in the cut-flower industry do not always notice they have medical problems, which tend to manifest later in life. Others, like one young mother at a community clinic held by the Centre for Studies and Consultation in Health (CSCH), cannot hold a pen straight and exhibits other disorders. But she continues working with cut flowers to make ends meet.

Nut 'graph: Dr. Jaime Breilh of the CSCH says they first thought poisoning through acute pesticide exposure was making cut-flower workers ill. As they studied the issue, however, they learned low-dose chronic exposure to pesticides caused the problems.

Imagine an article with this lead just before Mother's Day or Valentine's Day. At first, the reader might think it is another typical "love" article but would quickly see how it goes beyond the usual clichés and offers fresh insight. As the reader gets to the end of the first paragraph suddenly everything Mother's Day or Valentine's Day stands for has been stood on its head. The flowers we send to show our love could be making people sick? If this is something the reader did not know, then this information captures the attention of the reader and keeps him or her reading on.

Of course it drives the advertising department crazy as they are trying to sell flower ads around these special occasions, but that is not the editor's problem. The editor wants to enlighten readers.

While this article could appear in a newspaper, it could also appear on the website of a non-governmental organization that is promoting particular social causes. How the article unfolds in a newspaper might be different than how it unfolds on a non-governmental organization (NGO) website—the newspaper would have to include any contradictory points of view, for example. But the same lead could be used in the paper or on the website.

Scene-Setter Lead

Scene-setters open with description. They may contain some action, but the main point is to create a stage on which action can unfold, or to give a sense of place necessary to the focus of the story.

A woman with tormented eyes talks to herself as she plays a battered piano in Ward D's dayroom. Other psychiatric patients shuffle on the beige linoleum or stare from red-and-green vinyl chairs. A bank of windows opens to a fenced courtyard. Outside ... .

Significant Detail Lead

The article this next lead is taken from explored the continuing influence of communism and central planning on the operation of the shipyard and the economy of Poland. The statue of Lenin—hidden, but still in the neighborhood—perfectly symbolized the story's central theme and illustrates the use of a significant detail to craft a lead.

Hidden beneath a heap of inner tubes in a tiny storeroom on an island in the middle of the Vistula River is the statue of Lenin that stood for decades inside the Gdansk Shipyard.

To Question or Not to Question?

Some editors ban question leads, reasoning readers want answers, not questions; however, question leads occasionally work particularly, but not exclusively, for sports stories.

What's black and orange and the worst nightmare for teams headed to the state football playoffs?

The answer to the question is, of course, the local football team; its uniform is black and orange.

Leads that start with questions often fail because they do not perform the basic function of a lead—stating the central theme that organizes and explains the entire story. Furthermore, readers might resent frivolous questions when they want news. Still, some stories deal with fundamental questions. So, a question lead can be appropriate.

Profile Lead

Below is an example of a profile lead, followed by a quote and a transition. It may seem like a poster child lead, but the person in the lead does not represent the many, at least not in this article. The article is a profile that focuses on the lead character. The person in the lead could be used as a poster child, but then the article would be different—it would expand beyond the lead character. As you will see, there is a nut 'graph to transition from the lead to the body of the profile.

Lead: Paul Lima considers himself successfully retired from reality. He took a one-year sabbatical from Georgian College in Barrie, Ontario, where he worked as a continuing education program manager, and never returned. Instead, he moved to Toronto and launched a freelance writing business.

That was over 18 years ago.

"I could not see myself going back to work, not to a real job, after a year of freedom," said Lima who writes about technology and small business issues for The Globe and Mail, National Post, CBC.ca and a number of other publications.

Nut 'graph: While he now considers himself successfully retired from reality, success, as he defines it, did not come overnight. For the first three years, while working as a freelance writer ...

Notice in the first line how we give away the ending: Paul Lima considers himself what? "Successfully retired from reality." Then we give a little background information: here is where he was, here's what he did. However, even though we've given the ending away, we build some suspense using the transition line: "For the first three years, while working as a freelance writer ... " In other words, the fairytale has a happy ending, but we are going to go through freelance writing Hell to get there.

This type of lead or opening is often used in books and movies too. The book or movie starts with the ending, but the real story is in how you get to that ending.

Based on the lead/transition, readers know that they will experience the lessons that allowed Paul to successfully retire from reality. In that way, the transition holds the attention of readers. The hope, of course, is that the lead captures the attention of readers who are interested in freelance writing or people who have started their own small businesses.

Will we interview any other sources? If we want others who know Paul to talk about him we will. And that could make for a more interesting article. At the same time, this article could simply focus on Paul from his point of view (his story told to the writer). It all depends on where the article will be published and what the writer has negotiated with the editor. In other words, it depends on what is known as the slant or angle of the article.

Of course, as mentioned, if the article is about the struggles of freelance writers and what they have to do to achieve success in general, using Paul as the poster child, other writers and perhaps some industry experts will be interviewed. And if the article is about marketing a small business, using Paul as the poster child, then other business owners and marketing experts will be interviewed.

But this is a profile about Paul. Once you have a lead/transition like our profile lead above, it's all over but the writing. Add three or four hellish experiences. Tell some success stories. Mix in a few key quotes. Stir in lessons learned. Conclude with a final quote and comment, and you have baked a soft article.

Journal Exercise

Before we look at a few more leads, it's your turn to write a soft article lead. As always, feel free to do your own thing if you are working on an idea that you want to pitch to a publication or for work. At the same time, if you are looking for something to write about, the *Ordinary People* scenario below might be of interest to you.

Ordinary People

Pretend you are writing for *Ordinary People* (a fictional magazine): "At *Ordinary People*, we believe ordinary people are extraordinary."

Interview an ordinary person—a relative or friend, or your butcher, baker or candlestick maker—and find something that makes that person *extraordinary*. Then write a lead and nut 'graph.

You should know the person you interview will probably not consider himself or herself extraordinary. It's your job, through your interview, to find out what is extraordinary about that person. The extraordinary element might involve the person's entire life; it might involve one element of the person's life or one incident in the person's life. It's up to you to discover the extraordinary in the ordinary person you interview.

You'll do this through:

- Questions you choose to ask
- Listening closely to what the person has to say

- Asking for details and clarification on the things the person says
- Absorbing all that you have heard
- Writing your lead from the point of view (angle or slant) that says there is something extraordinary about this particular ordinary person

Before you start your extraordinary people interview, explain you are doing this as part of a learning experience, not for publication. Try your best to get organized but do not fret if you are not sure what questions to ask. Plunge in and have fun. Once you complete the interview, write your lead. **Note:** if the person is truly extraordinary and you decide to pitch a query to an appropriate publication, make sure you get permission from the person you interviewed first if you told the person that the work you were doing was not for publication.

Write your soft article lead before you read on.

Not Quite a Poster Child

There are so many soft articles online that I don't want to flood this book with examples. I will, however, include several here by way of example. I encourage you to look online for other non-news or soft articles. Look at your local newspaper and differentiate between hard news (*W5* leads) and soft news with leads similar to those in this book. Look also at online publications such as *The New York Times, Toronto Star, Time, Salon, Huffington Post* and others. If you have a company news magazine or employee website, read some of the articles posted there. Are there hard news articles and other articles that profile co-workers, clients, business accomplishments? How do they start? Where does the lead take you (or not, if ineffective). Read once for pleasure or to absorb the information presented, then read two times analytically to learn.

But allow me to give you a couple of concrete examples. To start, here is a soft lead from a long service article (two thousand words) on adaptive technology. Service articles provide a service—usually to inform and educate. There generally is no hard news related to a service; however, they can be inspired by a bit of news—a new breakthrough in technology, a new health study and so on. Most often, though, they are inspired by an editor or writer who feels readers of a particular publication, newsletter, blog or website would benefit from the information in the article.

The lead below may seem like a poster child lead or a profile lead, but the person in the lead does not represent the many, and he disappears from the article because the article is not a profile about him. The lead character is there to represent the theme of the article and engage the reader by putting a human face on something that might otherwise be kind of dry. I've included the transition out of the lead (the nut 'graph) and the end of the article too so you can see how the article comes full circle.

Lead: Kevin Huber can differentiate between intense light and dark shadows. Other than that, he sees nothing. Legally blind since birth, Kevin can navigate through his word processing package as fast as any computer user I've seen.

Kevin, 37, has his Masters in Science from Guelph University and works as a client support representative for Microcomputer Science Centre in Mississauga. He tests computer systems and software intended for use by visually challenged persons and shows instructors how to train disabled persons on computers.

The day I met him, Kevin was typing a report into his computer. While he cannot see the keys, he can touch type on his standard keyboard. And while he cannot see his computer screen, he hears what others see thanks to his IBM Screen Reader and speech synthesizer—two tools that translate visual information into audible information.

Kevin's dark, deep-set eyes almost twinkle when I ask him if he can imagine life without computers. "I don't have to imagine it. I lived it," he says and he vividly recalls his university days when typing a 500-word essay was a chore.

Kevin is one of many physically disabled persons who successfully use adaptive technology to adjust computers to their particular challenge.

Nut 'graph: As slanted sidewalks, or curb cuts, are used to make streets more accessible to mobility challenged persons, adaptive technology, or electronic curb cuts, are used to make computers more accessible to physically challenged persons.

Physical challenges can be divided into three categories—visual, hearing, and mobility. Visual challenges range from reduced visual acuity to total blindness. Hearing challenges range from slight loss of hearing to deafness. And mobility challenges range from impaired movement of hands and arms to only limited movement of the head and lips ...

Who reappears fifteen hundred words later, at the end of the article? Why Kevin, of course.

While advances in adaptive technology make computers more accessible for the disabled, access can still be a difficult and frustrating experience. Huber knows that first hand. But while he sometimes lags behind non-disabled computer users when learning new programs, he is not afraid to play with the new programs.

"I get into a lot of trouble others don't get into, but I learn more too."

Huber's advice to anybody thinking about entering the world of computers? "Embrace it with an open mind," he says because computers enable the disabled to participate in learning and employment experiences that may otherwise be closed to them.

If the article were a profile focused solely on Kevin and his accomplishments, he would not have disappeared. But the article was meant to provide a service—to inform physically challenged individuals and their employers of the computer "curb cut" options available. Kevin reappears to complete the circle: to connect the end of the story with its beginning. It is the payoff or reward, so to speak, for the reader. It makes the reader say, "Oh yeah, I remember why I started reading this." By closing the circle and bringing the reader back to the beginning, it makes the reader feel good or helps reinforce what the reader has learned.

Does all of this sound manipulative and premeditated? It is. Writing is a conscious act. You choose the words, sentences and paragraphs. You choose what information to put in and what to leave out, when to quote, when to paraphrase, and when to ignore what somebody has told you. You choose where to start and how to end your article.

The more you read and analyze other articles, and the more you write, the more natural it becomes. I was tempted to say "the easier it becomes" but it's never easy. If it became easy, then everybody would do it. It is definitely a craft, something you need to learn and practice.

One-Person Profile

Now, I'd like to take look at a full soft article that focuses on one person, television writer Sugith Varughese.

Sugith is successful in his field. His success would be of interest, one would assume, to others who write for film and television. (If we're going to be honest, we might say that his success and profile in a screenwriters' magazine might make other writers a tad jealous, but I think you get the picture: this article about a television writer would probably not be of interest to a doctor, lawyer, bricklayer or candlestick maker—unless any of them aspired to write for film or television.)

Headline: The Writing Warrior

"Writers must be warriors," says Sugith Varughese.

If any Canadian writer can say that, Varughese, 44, can. He has his black belt in karate and has earned his black belt equivalent in writing for television in Canada.

"There's a unwritten rule in karate when you are doing kata, ancient pre-arranged demonstration routines, that if you think you made a mistake, keep going ... I think that applies to writing," he says. And the award-winning writer has kept going since he wrote an episode of *The Phoenix Team* for CBC in 1979.

Earning a living is one battle the writer as warrior faces, says the India-born Varughese who moved to Canada when he was one.

Varughese comes from long line of doctors and, as the first-born son of a neurosurgeon, he was expected to become a doctor. But he showed an interest in drama and became the first pre-med and drama double major at University of Saskatchewan. However, he never did get around to attending medical school.

Armed with his BA summa cum laude in theatre from the University of Minnesota, his MFA in film from York University and a stint at the Canadian Film Centre, Varughese pursued his writing career.

He has been writing professionally for almost 25 years and his credits include the animated comedy, The Blobheads, Global TV's Blue Murder, the Jim Henson production, Fraggle Rock, as well as CBC movies, television and radio shows. Last year, his NFB animated short series, *Talespinners*, won a Black Film and Video Award for best short film and a Writer's Guild of Canada Top Ten award.

Still, the acclaimed writer does not earn his living full-time at the keyboard.

Varughese has choreographed an entertainment industry kata involving three moves: writing, directing (mostly industrial and corporate videos) and acting—with recent appearances on CBC's *An American in Canada.*

"I'd rather do that than work as waiter and a writer," says Varughese who sees the three jobs as related. "To me they are all story telling." But he finds writing the most difficult. "Directing is fun and acting is easy. Writing is hard [because] you start with nothing."

Rather than flaunting his triple-threat abilities, Varughese has separate resumes for writing, directing and acting. He says producers do not want to hire directors who write, fearing they will tamper with the script. Nor do they want writers who direct, fearing they will tamper with the directing. And casting directors do not want to recommend actors who write or direct fearing they will be difficult on set.

Varughese does not have to work hard to hide his talents. Like many successful entertainment industry professionals, he is not a household name, although his mother is convinced that her son, who has appeared in over 70 movies and television shows, would have been on David Letterman by now if he had worked in the US, he says with a chuckle.

"I do not aspire to stardom. I aspire to work. I'm a working actor and a working writer and a working director," he says. And his work as an actor and director allows him to "avoid writing for shows I don't care to watch."

As a writer, he attempts to craft scripts that directors can interpret, he says. Harold Pinter screenplays are minimalist, almost like haiku, but have tremendous evocative power, he points out. "You read the script and see the movie in your head. That's what writers should aspire to produce."

He takes pride in crafting the story but understands that he has to hand over his script to a director whose vision may not be in sync with his. "That's part of the joy and pain of being a scriptwriter," says Varughese.

In addition to directing, auditioning and writing for television, Varughese also works to kick-start his own projects. *Best of Both Worlds* (1985), his first movie script for CBC, dealt with the experience of "brown people" in Canada, but overall Varughese finds it difficult to raise money for films that come from the heart of his experiences. However, successful movies like *The Guru* and *Hollywood/Bollywood* may portent an attitudinal change in the industry, he says.

Varughese is currently discussing several script ideas with British producers. He finds them much more open to "mainstream movies and ideas with brown people who are funny, but not victims."

They are able to take risks because British films can be profitable by doing well in Britain. On the other hand, few Canadian films can make money domestically. That leads to complex co-production arrangements and the watering down of made in Canada stories, he says.

When Varughese feels frustrated by the constraints of the entertainment industry in Canada, which he does at times, he takes a deep breath and counts his successes. If that doesn't shake the feeling, the warrior takes to the mat and battles away his frustration by performing his intricate black belt karate katas.

Notice how the lead—in this case the first line of the article or a one-line lead—establishes two themes: writers and warriors. Since this is an article that appears in a screenwriters' magazine, writers is understandable. For the warrior theme to work, it must somehow be related to both Sugith *and* to writing. Otherwise, what's the point. Also, notice how the lead, again the first line, is a direct quote—something I suggested that you avoid in leads (in the tips below). Thank goodness, I say there are exceptions to the rule!

Notice also how the nut 'graph, or the second paragraph, does not have our standard *W5*. Although if you look closely, you will see a *who, what* and *where*. It's just not very newsy, nor does it have to be for a profile of a person. Finally, when you get to the end of the article, ask yourself what recurs to bring us full circle and reinforce the themes of the article.

Quoting Versus Paraphrasing

Before you move on, read the article again with quoting versus paraphrases in mind. Some writers think you have to quote an interviewee every time you convey something you've been told. That is not the case. You should only quote the most interesting statements the interviewee made (interesting and, of course, appropriate to the slant and theme of the article). Anything else that the interviewee has told you that you want to use, you can paraphrase. In other words, you don't have to use the interviewee's words. You can sum them up and simply add "he said" or "he says"—depending on the style used by the publication—before or after the paraphrase, as in the example in the second line of this paragraph:

> Rather than flaunting his triple-threat abilities, Varughese has separate resumes for writing, directing and acting. He says producers do not want to hire directors who write, fearing they will tamper with the script. Nor do they want writers who direct, fearing they will tamper with the directing. And casting directors do not want to recommend actors who write or direct, fearing they will be difficult on set.

Notice how, in this example, the paraphrase is used to establish where Varughese was born and how old he was when he came to Canada:

> Earning a living is one battle the writer as warrior faces, says the India-born Varughese who moved to Canada when he was one.

You don't even have to use the "he says" when paraphrasing. Think about it: unless you are writing a first person article, everything in your article comes from someone or something. If you had to attribute everything, you'd have "he says" or "according to" after every sentence. The writer did not know any of the information below until he interviewed Varughese. But we don't see "he said" used once in this paragraph because it is simply filling in the back story:

Varughese comes from a long line of doctors and, as the first-born son of a neurosurgeon, he was expected to become a doctor. But he showed an interest in drama and became the first pre-med and drama double major at University of Saskatchewan. However, he never did get around to attending medical school.

Armed with his BA summa cum laude in theatre from the University of Minnesota, his MFA in film from York University and a stint at the Canadian Film Centre, Varughese pursued his writing career.

Also, as you read it again, ask yourself if the article flows logically, moving you from the beginning, through the body of the article, to a clear end. Logically does not mean in chronological order. It means that the various points made in the article should connect and build to an ending that puts an exclamation mark, or at least a strong period, on your story. In other words, when you are writing profiles and soft articles, the editor should not be able to simply lop off the last couple of paragraphs to make it fit. The editor would have to nip and tuck at various places in the article to reduce word count.

Note: if an editor asks you for seven hundred and fifty words, do not file nine hundred or more words. File seven hundred and fifty words, plus or minus five percent. Otherwise, the editor might lop off huge chunks of the article, but only after lopping off your head. If the editor assigns you seven hundred and fifty words and you truly feel you have a story that is worth more (or fewer) words, discuss it with the editor before filing your story.

There are a couple more articles in Appendix I for your review. When reading them, look closely at the lead, the flow of the article from lead to conclusion, when and how interviewees are quoted versus paraphrased and when (if or how) the author seems to be drawing conclusions. Does the author do this in an overt way, injecting himself into the article? Or does he do this subtly, picking up on research information that has been gathered (from website, research sources or third parties)?

Awkward Lead

Leads tend to become awkward when you engage in the overloading of facts—names, numbers and other information. Overloading can easily confuse the reader.

> Dalton McGuinty, the premier of Ontario, today announced he would formally protest what he describes as the decision by the federal finance minister, Jim Flaherty, made on October 16, to not meet the obligations of the $1-billion Ottawa-Ontario Fiscal Accord negotiated between Ontario and Ottawa by Ralph Goodale, former federal finance minister in Paul Martin's short-lived minority government that was swept from office by the Conservatives in part on a platform to resolve the fiscal imbalance. Flaherty denies the allegation that he is….

Who did what? *When? Where? Why?* At this point, most readers would be saying, "Who cares?"

Lead-Writing Quick Tips

Here are a few quick tips to help you write leads.

Length: News lead: twenty-five to fifty words. Soft leads and feature-style leads can range from twenty-five to several hundred words or longer. Leads of several hundred words or longer are used primarily for feature magazine leads.

Attribution: You don't need to attribute any information in your lead to anyone you interviewed unless that needs to be clearly established. In most instances, you will not paraphrase anyone in the lead. As always, there are exceptions.

Quote leads: Starting an article with a quote rarely works. It has to be a spectacular quote to supersede the news or soft lead. Again, as always, there are exceptions.

Cliché leads: Dare I say it? Avoid them like the plague. "It is every mother's worst nightmare…" Leads like this are overused and are often used for trivial issues, issues that are not any mother's worst nightmare.

Numbers: Beware of using too many or you will overload the reader. Cite one side of a statistical battle in your lead. Set up the other side in the transition or further down in the article.

Talk to yourself: Read leads out loud. If they sound awkward or confusing, they are awkward or confusing. If you have to breathe half way through a sentence, the sentence is too long.

Journal Exercise

Now it's your turn to write a soft article. As always, feel free to do your own thing if you are working on an idea that you want to pitch to a publication or for work. At the same time, if you are looking for something to write about, you might want to carry on with the *Ordinary People* scenario in the previous journal exercise. Pretend that I am the editor and I have assigned you a seven hundred and fifty word article. No matter what you choose to write about, ask yourself the following questions:

- What am I writing about?
- What kind of lead should start the article?
- How long should the lead be?
- What is the theme and focus of my lead? Of my article?
- Who is my target reader?
- How does my theme/focus relate to what my reader wants to know about this topic?
- Who should I interview for this article? What background research is required?
- Should the article unfold in chronological order?
- If not, how should it unfold and what should I do to ensure it unfolds in a logical order?
- When should I quote? When should I paraphrase?
- Do I intrude or use someone else or other research to counter or support anything my main interviewee(s) has/have told me?
- How do I end the article?
- How do I ensure my theme is reflected in the ending?

Before you start to write your article, jot down a keyword or phrase that reflects your topic, and cluster it. Give it a good shot. Then review your cluster work and highlight points you feel you should make. Jot those points down or list them in Word. Once you've done that, put your points in order and add any other points and/or sub-points you think you should make. Once you have completed your outline, write your article from point to point until you complete your first draft. Review and revise (if required) your lead and ending once you have completed your first draft. Then review and revise the article from start to finish.

Note: You would, of course, do your clustering and create your outline after conducting any interviews and research. If you are the main source for your article, you'd still want to cluster your topic (consider this internal research) and jot down all the points you are going to cover in the article.

Write your soft article lead before you read on.

12/ Feature Articles and Leads

Feature articles can run anywhere from about fifteen hundred words at the low end, to ten thousand words at the high end. Most tend to run from two thousand to three thousand words. The longer features tend to be investigative articles that cover financial, business, relationship or political intrigue. Long form journalism, as longer features are often called, is beyond the scope of this book, as is interviewing people and writing investigative features. Shorter features, or less complex ones, can cover just about any topic worth writing about. They can be detailed service articles; they can cover new business, technological, medical or scientific developments; they can cover sports, entertainment, travel or other lifestyle issues. You name it, you can pretty much find a feature on it.

In this chapter, we will look at structuring a complex, multi-interview feature and we will then look at what might be called a *featurette*, a simpler, first person feature article.

First, a couple of overview comments on the feature lead.

The feature, even for a simple feature article, goes into more depth and detail than the typical soft lead and any *W5* news lead. While it can be a couple of paragraphs long, it can also run as long as a dozen or so paragraphs. It all depends on the overall length of the article, its focus and its complexity. Length aside, the feature lead should set the stage for the article by painting a vivid picture. It often introduces large themes, and establishes a conflict similar to fiction: man vs. man, man vs. nature, man vs. self, man vs. technology, and so on. The "vs." can be expanded to say "in conflict with" because most feature articles have conflicts, or include multiple points of view—the good, the bad and the ugly of a particular situation, one might say.

Show Versus Tell

Before we look at the feature lead in detail, I'd like to look at show vs. tell. Almost every writing student has heard this: Show, don't tell. It makes sense, but it's a principle that can be difficult to master.

Telling is the reliance on simple exposition:

Mary was an old woman.

Showing, on the other hand, uses evocative description:

Mary moved slowly across the room, her hunched form supported by a polished wooden cane gripped in a gnarled, swollen hand that was covered by translucent, liver-spotted skin.

Showing and telling as used above convey the same information—Mary is old. Telling states it flat-out. And showing? Read the example over and you will see it never states that Mary is old, yet leaves no doubt about it.

Now compare the two passages below.

Passage One

My father was cruel man. When I was a child, he often hurt me and caused me great pain. One day he beat me simply because I was crying.

Passage Two

The day I turned five I cried uncontrollably for some reason. I can't really recall why.

My father was deeply ensconced in the couch cushions, watching a football game and drinking beer. "Shut your friggin' yap, for christsake!" he shouted.

Maybe I was hungry; we had so little food then. Maybe I was sad because my mother had been in bed all day, again. For whatever reason, I continued to bellow. A second time my father shouted at me, but I cried on—an inconsolable prisoner in a rickety, splintered wooden playpen prison.

A third time: "If you don't stop, right now," he said, and paused to take a deep swig of beer, "I will give you something to cry about."

I did not stop. I could not stop.

My father did not tell me a fourth time.

He turned and threw the half-empty beer bottle at me, hitting me flush in the temple and silencing me until long after the ambulance arrived and took me to the hospital ...

In the second passage, I do not use the words "pain" or "hurt" or "cruel." But you see all of that and more. I suspect your reaction to the second passage is stronger than your reaction to the first because I am showing you what went on. When reviewers use terms like "vivid," "evocative" or "cinematic" to describe a novel, they mean the writer has succeeded at showing, rather than merely telling. Showing helps the reader see your images rather than filling in the blanks with images of their own, and it is used in creative writing and feature writing.

See Feature in a W5 Lead?

To start our foray into features, let's go back to the *W5*, the foundation of all articles. What I'd like you to do is to see if you can find the potential for a feature in the *W5* lead below (see journal exercise below). As mentioned, news stories are often written in inverted pyramid style. In the lead, the writer packs pertinent information or facts, embellished with little or no colour, and covers the story's five W's, as in this lead:

> More American teenagers are having babies, getting arrested or being killed by bullets each year, according to America's Children at Risk, a grim new portrait of American youth released yesterday. The year-long study said more than 6 percent of children under age 18—nearly 4 million—are growing up in so-called "distressed neighborhoods." Their future is gloomy.

Who, what, where, when and *why*. And a stunning conclusion: *Their future is gloomy*. All in an amazing 58 words:

Who: More American teenagers
What: are having babies, getting arrested or being killed by bullets each year
Where: America; distressed neighborhoods
When: each year; new portrait ... released yesterday
Why: growing up in "distressed neighborhoods"

I have to confess: I lied. This lead was, in fact, the *entire* article. It ran in the newspaper exactly as you see it above. No other information followed what I have called the lead. It is complete in itself because it answers the five W's. And yet, look at how it ends: "Their future is gloomy." Period. Full stop. As if there is nothing more to say. Or is there?

Maybe there was more to this story and the paper didn't have room to run it. Remember that news editors feel they should be able to cut a news story anywhere after the lead. While this two-sentence story is complete, I suspect you can imagine the potential here for a two thousand word human-interest feature based on the two sentences. With that in mind, I'd like you to try the journal exercise, below.

Journal Exercise: Finding Feature in the News

Imagine you've been assigned to write a two thousand word human-interest feature based on the two-sentence news article concerning American teenagers. You are writing this for the Life section of your local newspaper or for a magazine that explores social issues.

Answer the questions below to help you imagine the process you would go through to research a feature article:

- What is the local angle on this story? Is the future of teens in your city, town, state/province as "gloomy" or at all gloomy? Why? Why not?

- What would you read and who would you interview for background information on the state of teenagers in your community?

- Who else would you interview for this article to support the finding of the study?

- Would you look for a conflicting voice—a teen who has overcome difficult circumstances or a social worker who is optimistic, for instance?

- Where/how would you start the article? With the study? With a social worker or some other expert? With a teen who has had a baby, been arrested or been shot?

- How would you structure the article to draw the reader in and keep the reader reading?

- What points would you cover in your article? Make a quick list of ten or so major points you think would be included in your article.

- Would your conclusion state that "their future is gloomy" as the study concludes? Might you look for a counter-point, an 'unless' or 'however' statement: 'this is how things are and why they are and how they will remain unless/however … .' (As long as you have evidence that there is a counterpoint to this story.)

Answer the above questions before you read on.

W5 and Features

With complex feature articles, you will want to gather much more information than the *W5* before you start to write. Conducting in-depth interviews and doing background research goes beyond the scope of this book; however, I want to spend a moment looking at *W5* and feature articles. As you can imagine, there could be multiple *W5*s based on dissenting or contrary opinions and points of view when writing a feature article.

Your feature should have a nut 'graph, the article in a nutshell, after the lead. That nut 'graph will contain the dominant *W5*, or pertinent aspects of the dominant *W5*. However, it might not and probably will not contain all the *W*'s you encounter when conducting interviews and research. Before you write, in fact before you outline your feature, I suggest you do two things: list all the *W*'s (don't forget *how*) that pertain to your story and list the *W*'s that pertain to each person you interview.

As far as the *W*'s that pertain to your story, you should be able to do that if you think of your feature as news. Who are all the *who*'s in your article? *What* are their main issues, problems, opportunities and so on. *Where* do your *who*'s live or work; *where* do the *what* events take place? *When* did any and all of the important events and issues occur? *Why* did they happen? Or *why* are they happening? Or *why* did some important stuff not happen?

Again, you may have multiple *W*'s based on the different people you interviewed. Jotting them down before you outline and write will mean you can consciously determine the most important *W*'s in your story. It also means that you will be far less inclined to leave anything out, unless you feel it's not important. And you will become a more objective and impartial writer because you will have looked at your story from the perspective of all those you talked to.

Speaking of all those you talked to, they become your second set of Ws. Set up a *W5* for each person you interviewed. It might look something like this:

Who: who is this person (name, title, relation to the story)

What: what does, did, could, will this person do (in relation to the story); what knowledge and point of view does this person have

Where: where is, was or will this person be located

When: when did this person become important to the story

Why: why is this person important to the story

How: how does this person effect the story—make the main issue happen, reflect the main issue, move it forward, stop it, move it back

The above information will help you assess who you should use in your story, who you should leave out—and why. It will also help you get the facts right when referring to different people in your feature and give pertinent background information, as may be required, when you introduce different characters in your feature.

Notice the word "characters" above. That is who these people are, characters in your story. The *W5* helps you create a character sketch. That does not mean you are writing fiction. It means you will be able to make real people as real and as interesting as possible, as they should be based on their role in your feature.

Structuring a Feature

Let's think about the "American teenagers" feature again for a moment, and see how we might structure a feature article. Keep in mind that, to be effective, a feature article needs what might be called narrative tension—the kind of thing you'd find in a short story or other work of fiction. It is the tension—the conflict between people, a person and nature or technology, a person and the law or culture, a person and himself or herself—that keeps the reader engaged and reading.

If you were to write a lead for a feature article based on that news story, where would you begin the article?

I'd suggest that you'd want to lead with a poster child. As crass as it sounds, you'd want to find someone who represents the study—an American teenager who has had babies, been arrested, and shot, but not killed (as you couldn't interview the person if she was dead)., I am not being facetious. You'd use your poster child to create a human-interest lead that would capture the attention of your readers. The lead below is fiction. While it could be longer for a complex feature, it should give you a taste, of a lead that establishes a strong theme by painting a vivid picture. It also opens the article up to different points of view, as you will see.

Sheila Smith was only 14 when her first baby was born. It was December 23, 2009, a week before the resident of Harlem, in New York City, was arrested for shooting a drug dealer during a heroin deal gone bad.

She survived three years in jail, where she gave birth to her second child after being raped by a prison guard.

Two days after she was released from prison, Smith and her two children were shot dead by the drug dealer's girlfriend, in a revenge killing that has shocked a poverty-stricken neighborhood that thought it was no longer capable of feeling shock.

There are people in Smith's neighbourhood, ordinary people and neighbourhood leaders, who are saying enough is enough and are starting to work together to change the circumstances that have led to the seventh teen death is twelve weeks in the neighbourhood. Others are saying they would move tomorrow, if they could get out of the area.

You could then follow that human-interest lead, which broadens into action in the neighbourhood, with a nut 'graph summarizing the gist of the article and telling the readers more explicitly what the article is about and why it is being written. The nut 'graph, the transition from the lead to the body of article, would look a lot like the *W5* news lead we saw earlier:

More American teenagers are having babies, getting arrested or being killed by bullets each year, according to America's Children at Risk, a grim new portrait of American youth released recently. The year-long study said more than 6 percent of children under age 18—nearly 4 million—are growing up in so-called distressed neighborhoods.

But our story would not end there. This is, after all, a feature article. Following the nut 'graph you might use a quote:

"As our study indicates, their future is gloomy," says Anthony Times, the author of the report that was presented to a Congressional hearing on distressed neighborhoods in Washington last February.

While news articles sometimes (not always) take one point of view, feature articles invariable present opposing points of view. In other words, you want to support the findings of the study and then set up the reaction that demonstrates a conflict of opinion.

Supporting the study:

According to John Smith, New York City police chief, teenager youth crime is up 20% over the last two years and incarceration has increased just as dramatically. Teenagers are involved as low level drug and gun runners for major criminal organizations, he said, and they are frequently armed with guns and even assault rifles.

"We are seeing teens from rival gangs and criminal organizations involved in shoot outs in laneways and on street corners in neighborhoods that were once considered safe," said Chief Smith.

Echoing Smith's concerns, Amada Marshal, head of the National Organization of Youth, points out that teen pregnancy has been on the rise each year over the last five years. Many teens in urban centers who are getting pregnant have dropped out of school and are associated with gangs. "They are moving drugs for gang lords and are considered open targets by rival gang members."

If the study is accurate, you might not find anyone who opposed its result; however, you should be able to find people who oppose the sentiment behind it. Let's say you interview five or six social workers and clergymen. Some of them might support the study and say it's hell out there; others might not be as onside. Or they might think it's hell, but have ideas on how to make it less hellish, or even more heaven-like. You do not have to include everyone you talk to in your article, but you should look for appropriate balance:

Many social workers and clergymen say it does not have to be this way. Education, training and jobs—enough to provide a glimmer of hope—is all that is required to turn around the situation.

"Where pilot programs are in place in distressed neighbourhoods, we've seen a drop in teen crime, shootings and pregnancy," says Terry Munk, director of social work for the city of Detroit.

To alleviate this problem in urban centres nationally will take a concerted effort, and a whole lot of cash, and the government's coffers, at both the state and national level, are empty. Any funds that could be earmarked for additional services to assist inner city youth have already been committed to fight the debt and support the war against terrorism.

What comes next? It all depends on your *focus*. Simply put, that word, focus, is key. For instance, if you were writing this for a national magazine or major website that covered national issues such as this one, you might include any of the following:

- Comments from other clergymen and representative of social agencies, from other teenagers caught up in this bind and the parents of jailed, pregnant or dead teens.
- Comments from people who are trying to change the area; comments from those who feel all is hopeless and would leave today if they could.
- Background information on the human cost/burden.
- Background information on the financial cost.

- More comments from the author of the report.
- Comments from those representing various government agencies that should be funding programs, ideally juxtaposed against additional comments from the parents of the dead child and perhaps clergymen and spokespersons representing social agencies and so on.

On the other hand, if you were writing this for a local newspaper, profiling the neighborhood where Sheila (our poster child) lived and died, you could do the following:

- Talk to more teens in the neighborhood.
- Find an example of someone who bucked the trend and escaped the "gloomy" neighborhood.
- Give some background and history of the neighborhood: Was it always this way? When and why did it become this way?
- Use some reaction comments, farther down, from clergymen or social agencies.

Again, it all depends on the focus (angle or slant) of the article. You make your focus clear in your pitch or query letter to the editor (if you are a freelance writer); however, you always want to remain open to suggestions from the editor pertaining to the angle or slant as well.

Sample Feature Lead

Let's review a less complex feature, this one written in first person with no interviews required. Like any feature lead, the lead for even a simple feature goes into more depth and detail than the typical soft lead and any news lead. The sample lead below does not address a strong social or legal conflict or a major conflict between people, but I think you will agree that there is conflict there. It is mostly internal and, for the feature to be effective, it has to be resolved or end up worse than it is depicted at the beginning. In other words, something has to happen, there has to be change, for the article to be an article! (And yes, on rare occasion no change can be effective if readers were expecting major change.)

Here is the article from *Modern Dog*, a Canadian magazine on, well, dogs, and all things related to them. Again, the article is in first person. As the author, my assignment was to talk about my experiences—my love-hate relationship, you might say—with my dog, or more technically, my wife's dog. But notice where I start. Not in the present. Why? How does starting in the past capture (or does it capture) the attention of the reader and lure the reader into the article? I'm not asking you to like my lead; I am asking you to think about what I did and how, or if, it works for you. I will say that it worked for the editor, as she didn't touch a word.

Notice also how the lead is six paragraphs long. Long lead for the article, but then it's a long article, a feature, too. Notice also how the article flows logically and in a focused manner, or so I'd like to think. This is about my experience with dogs. I am not a poster child representing the experiences of the many. The article is about Kohl, the dog in question, and yours truly. If I were to write about how some people love dogs, and some people hate them, and some people hate dogs but come to love them, then I could have used something about Kohl and me as the lead, and played the part of poster child.

With that in mind, read the article below.

Note: I will interrupt the article now and then to comment on what's going on and why.

I was eight years old when my father came home with a dog. I don't know why he brought it home that Saturday in July. Nobody in the family had asked for one. Besides, my father was not a dog person. He was not even a pet person. We had two cats—Tipsy and Inky. He never fed them or cleaned their litter. Mostly he shooshed then away when they got underfoot.

But there he was, bringing home a yellowish dog of indeterminate breed and age.

My family—father, mother, older brother and sister, and younger sister—knew nothing about dogs. But I knew that a dog should have a name. I called the yellow stranger tied to a back-porch post, Max. I got Max a bowl of water and a plate of leftover spaghetti that he wolfed down, and I spent much of that day on the porch with him.

The next morning, our neighbour, Mrs. Rice, who was sitting on her back porch, overheard me coax Max off the porch into the yard to pee. (He hadn't used the newspapers we spread in the basement.) Mrs. Rice watched Max sheepishly sniffed around our postage-stamp sized yard before squatting to pee on a patch of weeds. "Maxine," Mrs. Rice laughed.

When my father came out to do some yard work, Mrs Rice said: "Your dog squats when she pees. Max is Maxine."

My father looked perturbed. He went into the house, made a phone call, came back out, coaxed the dog into the car, and left. And hour later he returned, without the dog. He had delivered Max—I never did call her Maxine—to relatives who lived in the suburbs because he didn't want her to put up with puppies. And that was that.

The lead ends here, with the unhappy ending of my short experience with my first dog. So I have used myself to paint a picture of a kid who was willing to play with and work with a dog, only to have the dog disappear on him. I'm setting the readers up, or so I hope, for what comes next, at least in terms of dogs and my relationship with them. I am not setting the reader up for my relationship with any other pets. Remember: focus!

"But what about the *W5* and nut 'graph?" You might ask.

Remember, it's not as simple in features as it is in news articles or soft articles. Still, we should be able to discern what might be called "the news" of the article:

Who: the author

What: short-lived relationship with a dog

Where: his home

When: when the author was eight

Why: it befuddles the author why his dad did this, although he knows why the dog disappeared—it was female

This information does not appear as a *W5* news lead or even as a standard nut 'graph. Instead, it is woven into the writing of the article. In addition, there are other characters in the lead and, as the article progresses, we will meet other *who*'s and see other *what*'s occur, at different *when*'s and *where*'s for different *why*'s or reasons. In short, the *W* information is there in a feature, but it's more complex and can often be found between the lines. Without it, you don't have an article.

And so the article continues:

Flash forward 35 years. My wife, Lyn, grew up with dogs and owned a Bouvier for 12 years before we met. When our daughter, Kyah, turned 9, Lyn announced it was time to get a dog. Kyah really, really wanted a puppy and Lyn said she was old enough to help take care of one.

I told Lyn all about Max. "You have a lot to learn," she said. "It will be fun. You'll get to walk him every afternoon." As a freelance writer who spends most of my day sitting, I know a walk a day is a good thing. But knowing did not equal doing. With a dog, I'd have motivation. So I agreed.

Notice the line, "It will be fun." That is what you might describe as foreshadowing. In fiction, foreshadowing hints (to the reader) about something that is coming up. In this case, you might call the line ironic foreshadowing. As you will see, it was not fun. What you do when writing soft articles is set up readers' expectations, and then meet them or dash them. If you are writing an article on five easy ways to stay in shape, I would suggest to you that you owe it to the reader to meet the expectations you establish. When you are writing something more personal, you have more latitude. That is not to say you have to dash expectations; that is simply to say you get to decide what you are going to do, and why. For instance, what would be the point of the article if Lyn said it would be fun and it was? There would be nothing gained.

I thought we'd go to the pound and pick out a small dog, ideally one that did not yap. Lyn had other ideas. "Trust me," she said when I asked her why she was visiting so many websites about dogs. She had embarked on a research project that lasted six months. Then one day she announced that we were on the waiting list for a Giant Schnauzer from Lindsay Leigh Kennels in Milton, Ontario. The breed didn't shed, liked exercise, had a good disposition and was good with children, she said. We were on the list so long that I all but forgot about the dog. Kyah, on the other hand, was as excited as a child waiting for Santa Claus.

Lyn went shopping for beds, bowls, dog books and leads. Finally, she announced that it was time to pick up the puppy.

You can imagine my shock when she brought home a 12-week-old Giant Schnauzer who was as big as many full-grown dogs. And his paws were huge. "He has to grow into them," said Lyn. "Just how big does he get?" I asked. "Pretty big ... "

I soon learned a bit about dogs.

I think it is fair to call the last line above an understatement. Kind of like the "it will be fun line" it uses irony (my wife would call it "sarcasm") to tell the story. Again, setting up expectations and then going from there as the story unfolds in a logical, thematic manner. By the way, if you think "fun" that isn't, and learning a "bit" that is actually a lot, are not thematically connected, then you need to study poetry. You don't have to write poetically, but you need to know that, in poetry (and in advertising), opposites belong in the same theme set. So black and white would belong in the same set; hot and cold would too. Of course red and green would as well, as would hot and humid. Using words, phrases or concepts that belong in the same thematic set become the glue that hold the story together and help it maintain focus and unfold in a logical order. This works in a similar manner to news stories. In news stories, ensuring that you can connect all points in the story in some way to the lead helps you to set up and meet expectations and to ensure your story unfolds in a focused and logical manner.

> Evidently, a puppy sleeps, wakes, walks two feet from its bed and evacuates! The key to dry floors, Lyn said, was to be with the dog when it woke up, and move it gently but swiftly out the door. "Dogs don't like to soil their home. Soon he'll ask to go out," she said. However, it takes a certain knack to know when your dog is going to wake so you can be there. Lyn had that knack; I did not. But, to Kohl's credit, he learned to walk to the door and wait to be let out. And, to his credit (and Lyn's dog rearing skills), he never once defecated in the house.
>
> Although cats require love and care, they are independent creatures and I was totally unprepared for the degree to which the puppy was dependent on us for food, water, bathroom breaks, walks, baths, brushing and grooming.
>
> The first year with Kohl was hell.

I don't go on about this hell, but I'd like to think I set up the reader to arrive at this point—not by moaning and complaining, but by being understated. And it is that understatement that makes the above "hell" line even more effective. Again, not asking you to agree with me. It's all subjective. But I am telling you what I was thinking and what my editor liked about the story. And the editor is the gatekeeper between you, the author and the readers of the publication.

The article goes on:

Generally, right after a bath or a good brush, Kohl loved to romp through a bush full of burrs in the High Park off-leash area, or he would gleefully roll in dead, ripe carrion. And suddenly it was time for another bath or brush.

Then there was the chewing.

Because Lyn and I both work from home, we didn't crate Kohl (not that I knew it was an option). Kohl got so used to one or both of us being there that when we tried to go out to dinner or a movie, he would find something expensive to chew. Or he would chew on an inexpensive little nothing that would lead to an expensive veterinarian bill. And this after we had, in my mind, dog proofed the house.

And there was the walking.

Notice the one-line paragraphs used in this story? If you haven't noticed them, go back and look. See how they tend to punctuate (almost like an exclamation mark) a theme and/or sentiment. This helps keep the reader reading by having them think, although it might be subconsciously, Aha, I get it! If the reader has moments like this, it keeps the reader engrossed in the story.

I admit it, when Lyn said I'd have to walk the dog every afternoon, I did not think she meant every afternoon, let alone sometimes afternoons and evenings. I did not think it meant that I'd have to walk the dog when it rained or snowed, or was hot or cold!

The walks were not the relaxing strolls I used to take. Instead, they became anxiety-inducing obligations. Kohl would more or less heel for Lyn, but not for me. Lyn would train him to heel in the morning, and by time I finished the afternoon walk she'd have to retrain him. Rather than take Kohl for a walk, I started to drive him to High Park—a five-minute walk from our house. I'd let him loose in the off-leash area and he'd romp with other dogs while I sat on a picnic table, pouting. Double-pouting if it was raining, snowing, hot or cold.

And do you think we could get Kyah, the daughter who had been pining— "please, please, please, I'll walk him and brush him and feed him"—for a dog, to walk him? Forget about it!

There was also the projectile doggy diarrhea at two o'clock in the morning, usually after Kohl had devoured some rather ripe dead thing in the park. To give Kohl credit (and I did not give him much credit) he'd whimper and wake us so somebody could take him outside, where he could explode without doing too much damage, other than to the lawn.

A dog owner might say, "So, what did you expect? He's a dog." I guess I expected a cat that barked. All I know is that I did not want a dog in our house, and I was beginning to express it quite vehemently—to the point where it was putting incredible stress on our family.

The turning point came one summer Sunday.

Ah ha! A *turning point*. Again, readers should read right through this without consciously thinking about what you are doing. But subconsciously, they should have a sense of anticipation—that things are going to get better, in this instance. In literature, it's called foreshadowing or setting up the reader for what is to come.

I forgot that all but one High Park entrance was close to vehicular traffic. Driving Kohl to his walk, I got stuck in a traffic jam, and then could not find a parking spot. A drive that should have taken me two minutes, took almost 45 minutes.

After abandoning my car in an illegal parking spot, I made it to the off-leash area where I sat on a picnic table and steamed. Kohl, on the other had, relieved himself, had a long drink and started to play with other dogs. The long, irritating drive over was in the past; it had not affected his ability to enjoy the present.

A cloud covered the sun momentarily, and something snapped. It was like the conversion of Saul on the Road to Damascus. I watched my dog—my dog—having great fun, and I decided that it would not hurt me to emulate him—at least in some ways!

The next day, I left my car at home and walked him—really walking him—along the off-leash paths in High Park. I started to look forward to the walks. If my schedule allowed it, I'd walk in the morning with Lyn, and still do the afternoon walk. I learned how to dress for the weather and discovered that I could be quite comfortable when the wind chill factor is minus 30-degrees. And I learned how to admire Kohl's zest for life and his unconditional affection—even if he still pulls on the lead.

There is no denying that, as the years went by, Kohl, who is now five, matured. But I matured too. I guess I had to meet him half way. After all, he is just a dog. A loyal, friendly, gentle—although large at 29 inches and 110 pounds—furry creature who wants to romp, eat, play with his friends and enjoy good long sleeps.

I swear he understands that he needs me around as much as I have come to want him around.

One day last summer, as Lyn, Kohl and I were enjoying a leisurely walk through High Park, I turned to Lyn and said three words I'm sure she thought she would never hear.

"Thanks for Kohl," I said. "Thanks for Kohl."

Can you see how the entire article, from start to finish, is focused on something—something that readers of *Modern Dog* could appreciate? Now if you've never owned a dog, especially if you are a cat person, you might not appreciate the article. That said, you are not the target reader. So what you write and the angle, slant or focus you take, as I have said before, depends as much on your reader as it does your topic. In other words, this is not an article that I'd write for, say, *Modern Goldfish*.

Note: Kohl was a magnificent dog. He died in February, 2013, a week before I finished the second draft of this book. He was almost twelve years old. He will be missed. (I don't mean to go on, but if you want to see him in a slide show, go to this YouTube link: www.youtube.com/watch?v=1whhQujSZNA.)

Journal Exercise: Write a Feature Lead

See if you can write your version of the "more American teenagers" lead. Conversely, see if you can find a big idea about which you'd like to write a feature article. It could be a complex story that might involve a fair amount of background research and a number of interviews. It could be a simpler, but long story, from your perspective or the perspective of one or two others.

Either way, try to write a detailed lead, one that targets a defined audience and transitions into the body of the article. You may have a nut 'graph; you may not have something quite as obvious. It all depends on your theme, angle and the complexity of the story you are trying to tell. Your lead should, however, capture the attention of the reader, set up the body of the article and lead the reader into the body.

The article itself, should you choose to write a full article, should contain tension and conflict. The writing should primarily show not tell. Just as the lead captures the attention of a defined target audience, the body should hold the interest of your audience.

This begs the questions: how defined should the audience be? The answer depends in large part on the publication. If you are writing for *Modern Dog* or *Modern Accountant* or *Modern Machinist* or *Modern Superhero* (I have made up the last three publication titles), you have a fairly well defined target audience.

If you are writing for a men's magazine or a women's magazine, you have a broadly based audience defined by gender—unlike *Men Pumping Iron* or *Women Pumping Iron* (again, fictitious titles—although such targeted publications exist)—which would appeal to men and women, respectively, interested in pumping iron (lifting weights).

Write a feature lead before you read on.

13/ Writing Media Releases

I wanted to include a chapter on writing media releases because well-written media releases are exceptionally focused documents, and they definitely use *W5* (*who, what, where, when,* and *why*) up front. In fact, if you had any doubts about the importance of knowing your *W5* before you write, the media releases presented in this chapter will help dispel those doubts. In addition, if you had any doubts about getting organized before you write, you will see how outlining your *W5* will help you write powerful openings that capture the attention of a well-defined target audience, or the gatekeeper—the editor—of your defined audience.

Finally, you will see how the major or most important *W5* elements are used in the headline, sub-head, opening paragraph, and quote paragraph of a media release.

Using the *W5* in several elements is like using the most important thing you have to say in a subject line of an email message, using it in your opening paragraph and confirming it in your closing.

In short, a modicum of repetition is your friend when it comes to writing media releases. If you have something important to say and you say it several times for effect in a media release, that is not being redundant. It is placing emphasis where it should be placed, something that well-written media releases do effectively. But before we look at how media releases do it, let's define a media release.

Note: I cannot tell you everything you need to know about writing and issuing media releases and media advisories in one chapter. (If interested, you will find much more about this topic in my book, *How to Write Media Releases to Promote Your Business, Organization or Event.*)

What is a Media Release?

A media release is a formal one- or two-page document that a public relations agency or the marketing or communication department of a company (or non-profit organization) uses to pitch a newsworthy story to the media.

If the story is of interest, the release may appear as written, either in whole or in part. If the story, however, is seen as particularly newsworthy, an editor or reporter may call the contact person (listed on the media release) to set up an interview for more information.

If the editor feels the release is not newsworthy, or if she has no space for it, then the release will not be used. The sender has no control over this. However, if the sender targets a concise, well-written, informative release to the right editors at appropriate publications or media outlets (print, broadcast, online) it improves the chances of the release being picked up, in whole or in part, or in having a reporter call to conduct an interview based on the release. With that in mind, the contact listed on the release must be prepared to speak to the media about the issue raised in the release.

Why Bother with Media Relations?

Consumers regard advertising with a degree of scepticism. Yet, if they read the same message in a newspaper or magazine article (or hear it during a news program on television or on the radio), they are more inclined to believe it or seek out further information. This can have a positive impact on your bottom line or on your social or political cause. In addition, media relations offer a cost-effective way for organizations to get their messages out to their community and stakeholders. Media releases do not replace marketing and advertising; however, they should be used in conjunction with marketing and advertising plans.

Sample Media Release

Before we go any further, let's look at a sample media release.

WIDGET CO. PRODUCES 1 MILLION WIDGETS IN 5 YEARS
Production Achievement Surpasses Expectations, Maintains Focus on Quality:
One Millionth Widget Rolls Off Line August 1

Brampton, Ontario July 28, 2012 – Widget Co. Inc. today announced that its one-millionth Widget will roll off the assembly line on August 1, 2012, at its production facility in Brampton, Ontario. Widget Co. experienced exponential growth, exceeding industry expectations, to reach this remarkable milestone in five short years.

"We are extremely proud of our employees, the people who put quality into every Widget produced by Widget Co. They are the people who enabled Widget Co. to produce our one-millionth Widget in five years, growing from a production run of under 25,000 Widgets in year one to over 350,000 this year," says Tom Kohl, CEO and Founder of Widget Co. Inc. "While our growth has been remarkable, we never waivered from our commitment to quality and innovation," Mr. Kohl added.

Widget Co.'s real time online customization and ordering process, its innovative ISO 9000-certified continuous improvement production techniques, and its just-in-time delivery methods have allowed the company to grow in a planned, cost-effective manner while delivering quality products to Mega-Widget manufacturers across Canada and the United States.

The Widget Production Association of Canada (WPAC), at its Annual General Conference held last month in Toronto, lauded Widget Co. for its impressive and unprecedented growth in Widget production. "Widget Co. has contributed to the growth of this industry as a whole, while focusing on quality," said WPAC president, Sarah Wise.

- ### -

About Widget Co. Inc.: Founded in 2005, privately held, ISO 9000-certified Widget Co. Inc. produces high-quality Widgets used in the manufacturing of Mega-Widgets at manufacturing plants across North America. Widget Co. employs 57 engineers, production workers, and sales and administrative staff at its Brampton, Ontario, production facility.

For More Information: Mary Press: 905-555-1212 or mp@widgetco.com

W5 in the media release

Let's deconstruct the media release so we can review *W5* components used in the release:

Who: Widget Co.

What: Produces one million widgets

Where: At its plant in Brampton, Ontario

When: In five years; August 1

Why: There are often multiple "whys" in media releases; see below for an analysis

What are the *why's* here? There is "why announce this?" The company is hoping for exposure in newspapers and magazines that potential clients read, but can't say that. Then there is "why is this news?" Other companies may have produced a million widgets, but no one has done it faster. The media loves records, so that is why this is news, for the right publications. You need to be clear on your *why's* before you can determine your *why* priorities, including which whys you will and will not address.

The *W5* is the foundation of media releases, even though there are often other components you have to add to releases (as with most other documents). For instance, notice the emphasis on quality. Without overtly saying so, this release could be issued to assure possible customers that widgets can be mass produced while maintaining quality. As a writer—and this applies to anything you write—you need to know what you want to stress and you need to stress it by weaving it into your writing in an unobtrusive manner while making sense based on the content and context of your message. In the Widget release, the news is the production achievement; however, the company needs its target market to know that this was done without compromising quality

So think beyond the *W5* for other aspects you have to address (this will often be dictated to you by a manager or, if you are a freelance writer, by a client), and weave them into your release in a clear, concise, coherent and focused narrative.

Finally, when you are writing articles, the editor will generally write the headline and sub-head. If you are writing media releases, that is something you will do. You will write the headline and sub-head, weaving in the most important *W5* elements.

Media Release Components

Let's take a closer look at the components of the media release. Notice, as well, how the major aspects of the *who, what, where, when* and/or *why* elements are repeated in the headline, sub-head line, opening paragraph, and quote paragraph.

Headline: WIDGET CO. PRODUCES ONE MILLION WIDGETS IN FIVE YEARS

Sub-head: Production Achievement Surpasses Expectations While Maintaining Focus on Quality: One Millionth Widget Rolls Off Line August 1

Dateline: Brampton, Ontario July 28, 2010

Opening paragraph: Widget Co. Inc. today announced that its one-millionth Widget will roll off the assembly line on August 1, 2010, at its production facility in Brampton, Ontario. Widget Co. experienced exponential growth, exceeding industry expectations, to reach this remarkable milestone in five short years.

Quote paragraph: "We are extremely proud of our employees, the people who put quality into every Widget produced by Widget Co. They are the people who enabled Widget Co. to produce our one-millionth Widget in five years, growing from a production run of under 25,000 Widgets in year one to over 350,000 this year," says Tom Kohl, CEO and Founder of Widget Co. Inc. "While our growth has been remarkable, we never waivered from our commitment to quality and innovation," Mr. Kohl added.

Note: Writers of media releases don't take the time to interview subjects hoping for a solid, focused quote. Rather, it is the norm for the writer to make up the quote and then ask the spokesperson to review it, revise it as may be required, based on corporate policies and priorities, and approve it.

Support paragraphs: A series of, background paragraphs followed by hash marks (###) that indicate the end of the portion of the release you hope will be published.

About paragraph: About Widget Co. Inc ... .

Contact information: For More Information: Mary Press: 905-555-1212 or mp@widgetco.com

Focus is Key

As with any writing, an effective media release should focus on one aspect of business—something newsworthy that will turn the crank of an editor or reporter, the gatekeepers who can report on your news so that your target audience will read about you, your firm, your (or your company's) accomplishments in newspapers, magazines or online journals.

Just as you would focus on content, you should also focus your media contacts. In other words, don't send your business news media release to the food editor (unless you are a food company). Don't send your theatre production announcement to sports reporters (unless your play is sports related). Don't send your enterprise software announcement to magazines for women like Chatelaine or Ms. (unless it will allow companies to address issues related to women).

In short, you should have a clear idea of what you want to say (message focus), to whom you want to say it (target audience), and which media outlets will reach your target audience. Then you should write what you have to say, following the standard media release format presented here. Doing all of that will increase your chance of a hit—having your release picked up and used by media outlets.

Closer Look at Leads

To capture the attention of the editor or journalist who receives your media release, the headline and sub-head line should contain the most important *W5* aspects; the lead or opening paragraph or two should contain the entire *W5*. With that in mind, here are several sample leads, followed by one more media release and a writing exercise. See if you can identify the *W5* in each.

Montreal, June 18, 2008 – West Jet announced today that it is extending its special first anniversary sale of one-way, $1 fares from Toronto to all of its Canadian destinations. A return flight at regular, low summer rates must also be purchased. Regular taxes and surcharges are extra.

Toronto, Ontario, Aug. 24, 2004 – Working Women Community Centre today announces that it was selected as the first Ontario site for Home Instruction for Parents of Preschool Youngsters, a school readiness program developed in Israel to maximize, through early intervention, the educational potential of young children in low-income families.

Toronto, Ontario, January 4, 2009—Paul Lima, a successful freelance writer, author and writing trainer, today announced the release of his tenth book, *How to Write A Non-fiction Book in 60 Days*. Available as a PDF file or trade paperback (www.paullima.com/books), *How to Write a Non-fiction Book in 60 Days* helps consultants, workshop leaders and others who aspire to write non-fiction books overcome the number one barrier to success—the lack of a planned approached to organizing and writing their books.

The following is one of my favourite leads because it packs so much information into one sentence. Okay, I am being sarcastic. The release packs way too much information into one sentence. Having said that, though, it may seem convoluted but if you read it slowly, it makes sense. Still, I would not write an opening that was this thick, shall we say:

Montreal, Sept. 20, 1998 – The Honourable Claude Drouin, Secretary of State (Economic Development Agency of Canada for the Regions of Quebec) and MP for Beauce, on behalf of the Honourable Jane Stewart, Minister of Human Resources Development Canada (HRDC), will participate in a commemorative tree-planting ceremony at the Commission scolaire de la Beauce-Etchemin of Saint-Georges, to commemorate 75 years of public pensions in Canada.

A final lead

Toronto, Ontario, June 15, 2009 – On June 23, Canadian Actor Online (CAO) celebrates 10 years of educating actors about the entertainment business in Canada, CAO (www.canadianactor.com) provides actors with networking and audition opportunities and a forum to promote themselves and their work. The website, established by veteran actor and ACTRA/Equity member Lyn Mason Green, also continues to combat fraud in the entertainment industry by educating its members on professional industry standards for actors, agents and employers.

I'll deconstruct the lead to make sure you see all five Ws.

Who: Canadian Actor Online (CAO)

What: celebrates 10 years of educating actors about the entertainment business in Canada

Where: Toronto, Canada, and—most important—www.canadianactor.com

When: June 23, 2009

Why: You might think the release has been issued because (why) CAO is celebrating its 10th anniversary. However, that is the what—what is happening—of the release. The why, from the perspective of aspiring and new actors is: "provides actors with networking and audition opportunities and a forum to promote themselves and their work; continues to combat fraud in the entertainment industry by educating their members on professional industry standards for actors, agents and employers." We can quibble over this. The important thing is that you, as the writer, know what your *W5* is in relation to your news and what your target audience wants to know about you.

Sample Media Release

Here is another sample media release for your perusal. Analyse it and find the *W5* in the lead. And then look at the headline and sub-head. Which aspects of the *W5* were used there? Were any aspects of the *W5* used in the quote paragraph , or expanded upon in the quote paragraph or any other paragraphs in the release? "Read," as Atwood said. Read analytically.

Youth Volunteer Association Puts Time on Charities' Side
Young People Bid Volunteer Time for Art to Support Charities on August 1
at YVA Silent Auction in Toronto

Toronto, Ontario July 15, 2009 – In a twist on the standard silent auction, young people can bid time in exchange for original art and help three local charities in need of volunteers at a Youth Volunteer Association (YVA) silent auction to be held in the lobby of the CBC building on August 1 from 7:00 PM to 10:00 PM.

Instead of bidding money, silent auction participants will bid time, in two-hour increments, for over 100 pieces of original art donated to the YVA silent auction by Canadian artists. The winning bidders will then donate their time to any one of three participating charities—the United Way, Canadian Cancer Society, and Salvation Army.

"Young people are often strapped for cash and charities are often strapped for volunteers. So this is a perfect match," said Jim James, YVA founder. "By encouraging youth to give their time to charities, we are letting them know they can contribute and make a difference, without reaching for their wallets. We are also fostering an important spirit of volunteerism."

Combined, the United Way, Canadian Cancer Society, and Salvation Army use over 5,000 volunteers contributing almost 500 million hours per year to a vast variety of activities that would not get done if it were not for volunteers.

"Driving cancer patients to and from chemotherapy appointments takes time, and if it were not for volunteer drivers, many cancer patients would have to rely on taxis or public transit. But too often they cannot afford cabs and they are too weak to take transit," said Mary Heart, president of the Canadian Cancer Society. "Volunteers are essential."

"We are pleased to participate in the YVA silent auction," she added. "It is an innovative way to boost volunteerism and to encourage young people to get involved with charitable organizations."

The doors to the silent auction open at 6:30 PM. Many of the contributing artists will be creating art during the event and popular indie bands Funk-a-delic and sPunk will perform. Admittance is free, but people are encouraged to bring canned goods and other non-perishable items for the Toronto Food Bank.

- ### -

About Youth Volunteer Association: Founded in 2000, the YVA (www.yva.com) is an independent, non-profit organization dedicated to encouraging volunteerism among people under 30. Over 10,000 YVA volunteers across Canada have logged almost one million volunteer hours since YVA's inception.

For More Information: Contact: Jean Roi: 905-555-1212 or jroi@yva.com

Breaking the Template

Occasionally, a media release will break the template. Often, this leads to a misfired release. But on occasion, a release will hit home when it breaks the template.

The president of KnetGolf wanted a light media release sent out. He wanted to break the template so he could cut through the clutter of the other releases out there. He was taking a chance but it paid off. It was around the time Blockbuster Video cancelled late fees so he played on that concept a bit and generated hits with newspapers and TV stations. Also, it was released in the very early spring, when the golfers are dusting off their clubs and dreaming of the first day on the greens. So it was a timely release.

The release is a bit long for my liking, but it is difficult to argue with success—it was picked up by several national and local newspapers. In addition, a couple of television news stations interviewed the president for news segments.

KNETGOLF Rents Golf Balls – from $5 per Dozen
Use them. Lose them. Don't return them. There's never a late fee.

Markham, Ontario, May 3, 2005 – Spring is in the air and golfers are getting twitchy as they wait to hit the fairways. Some golfers are looking wistfully at their expensive brand name golf balls, knowing that they will soon lose them. But others are not so wistful. They've joined over 50,000 golfers who last year rented golf balls for half price or less from North America's first and largest Internet golf ball rental outlet – KnetGolf.

With the price of golf balls topping over $65 per dozen, golf balls have become a costly expense. Most golfers purchase golf balls, play with them, lose them, or wear them out; and replace them with expensive new balls. KnetGolf's unique golf ball rental program, on the other hand, has made it easy for golfers to play with the latest and greatest balls on the market – for a fraction of what new golf balls cost at pro-shops or retail outlets.

"Does KnetGolf really rent golf balls? Not really," said Gary Shienfield, co-owner of the Markham, Ontario-based KnetGolf.com. "However, many of our customers say that shopping online at KnetGolf is like renting golf balls. They save big by purchasing half-priced golf balls from us. They use them, lose them and come back to KnetGolf for more balls!"

Golfers who rent their favourite golf balls directly from KnetGolf (www.knetgolf.com) enjoy the following benefits:

- Save up to 65% or more over the cost of buying new
- Choose their favourite golf balls from over 400 popular brands
- Free delivery by UPS with each rental of $100 or more
- Enjoy a 100% satisfaction guarantee

KnetGolf is the largest Internet supplier of recycled golf balls, distributing over 5,000,000 brand name golf balls annually, at up to 50% off, to customers across North America.

Instead of manufacturing golf balls and competing against the major brands for market share, KnetGolf crews recover golf balls at over 300 high quality golf courses, mostly in the southwest United States. The KnetGolf staff clean, sort, and package the recycled golf balls, and golfers get a significant break on the price of their golf balls.

"Because of our vast network, we acquire the best quality and best brands of golf balls for our ever increasing and very loyal customers. We sell the balls at substantial savings," said Mr. Shienfield.

"So, for the golfer who loses golf balls on a regular basis (and who doesn't do that?) buying from KnetGolf is just like a rental program. Only, you don't have to return the balls and there are no late fees!"

Golfers can choose from over 400 leading brands of golf balls, all sorted and packaged. Golf balls come in various grades including Mint, Grade A, Grade B, Range Balls, Refinished Balls, Coloured Balls, Ladies Balls, Low Compression Balls and High Compression Balls.

- # # # -

About KnetGolf: KnetGolf (www.knetgolf.com) is a privately held company that has been in business since 1995. Based in Markham, Ontario, KnetGolf is the home of the half-priced golf ball and sells over 5 million golf balls each year online, by phone, fax or mail order. Golfers across North America can choose from over 400 leading brands of discounted recycled and refinished golf balls.

For more information, contact: [Name, phone number, email address]

Newsworthy in the Eye of Media

To help you focus your media release writing, look at what the media considers newsworthy. Newsworthiness depends on the nature of your business and your community or target market. By *community*, I literally mean the community in which your business is located if your product, service or issue is of interest to the local community. In most instances, though, you have a defined target audience you serve or want to influence.

To score a hit, you have to focus your message and pitch it to the publications and media outlets that are most likely to use it. In other words, you have to define your community or target market and then find publications, broadcast outlets or websites and blogs that reach it.

For instance, local news is a priority for community newspapers and there tends to be space for announcements of events, meetings, classes and the like. Nearly all of this material is generated by media releases. Business-oriented briefs concerning expansions, contracts, promotions and employment opportunities are also newsworthy. If your release is of interest to members of a local community only, you need to find out who to contact at the community newspaper. Having said that, some companies and organizations have news that is of interest to many small communities. It is your job to track down the newspapers (and radio and TV stations) in those communities and find contacts. (More on finding contacts later in the book.)

Magazines, on the other hand, tend to specialize—entertainment, business, sports, fashion, hunting, fishing, women's issues, health and fitness, new age, computers, media and so on. You name a topic and you can find a magazine for it, just as you can find a website for it. There are, of course, subsections within these niches in magazines and on the web.

Most magazines serve a national community; some serve an international community. However, publications like the *New Yorker* or *Toronto Life* (and other city-specific magazines) serve specific cities. Although local magazines might tackle state/provincial, national or international events and affairs, they generally deal with some kind of local slant or angle. A very few, like the *New Yorker*, serve a local community primarily but are read by a larger international audience.

Trade magazines serve a particular industry or niche within an industry. For instance, there are numerous automotive trade magazines. Some are geared toward automotive manufacturers, while others are geared toward the retail end of the automotive business. Still others target parts manufacturers. For every industry and business sector, and almost every niche within every industry and business sector, there is a trade magazine. Your job is to find the publications that speak to your community.

Of course there are daily papers that tend to serve particular cities, and there are daily national publications such as *USA Today* and *The Globe and Mail* in Canada. And there are broadcast media that can be stratified by the communities—be they geographical or by particular interests, such a sports and business.

In short, you want to focus your content and the distribution of your release. Do not send your media release to every publication or broadcast outlet out there. That is a waste of your time and of the time of editors and reporters. Focus your message. Focus on contacts at appropriate media—the media that serves your target market.

Note: the same can be said for websites and blogs that carry news from third parties. Just because it's called the World Wide Web doesn't mean everybody in the world will be interested in your news. And it doesn't mean every website or blog will cater to people who are interested in what you have to say. So focus your writing and your distribution.

Journal Exercise: Write a Release

Now it is your turn to write. Review the two case studies on the next couple of pages and then follow these instructions:

- Pick one of the case studies.
- Refine the idea suggested to promote the event. (To what extent you refine the idea I will leave up to you. The goal is to write a clear, focused media release that appropriately reflects the company or organization and meets the stated purpose.)
- Outline your *W5* before you write.
- Write your lead—literally the first paragraph or two of your release.
- Write your headline and sub-head line based on your release.
- Add a quote paragraph.
- Write two or three other paragraphs to fill in any other pertinent details (make up any facts you might need to flush out the release).
- Include an "about" paragraph and contact information (as you see with the sample releases in this session).

Case Study A

The Canadian Apple Growers Association (CAGA) has hired your public relations agency to stage and promote an event in New York City. The purpose is to attract media attention to create public awareness of the Ambrosia apple.

The CAGA's goal is to boost sales of Canadian apples in the United States. Since the Ambrosia apple is not grown in the United States, CAGA feels this apple offers a unique marketing opportunity.

Background information: The Ambrosia apple is a chance seedling discovered in the early 1980s in B.C. It's now grown in B.C. and Ontario. It's a good-quality red apple that ripens in late fall. Its parents are Golden Delicious and Starking Delicious.

The fruit is medium to large in size with an attractive red blush and faint stripes on a cream or yellow background. It's crisp, sweet, low in acid, very juicy. It has a distinct, pleasant aroma and mild flavour. It's excellent eaten fresh or in fresh salads as the flesh is slow to oxidize (brown).

There is an Internet rumour that the apple has been used as an aphrodisiac.

The idea: To hold a Canadian-style fall fair in the Big Apple. The fair would run the first Saturday and Sunday in October in Central Park. It would include hay-rides, pony rides, an apple pie-baking contest, an apple pie-eating competition, free apple cider and balloons and, of course, free Ambrosia apples.

There would be music playing all day—fiddling and jug bands as well as folk music—and square-dances, including free square-dance lessons.

Your task: If you choose to work on this case, refine the event as you see fit. Outline your *W5* and write a release that will capture the attention and hold the interest of the media and, through the media, your target market.

When reading the case study, think about what you should leave in and what you should leave out of your media release. The release will be sent to food and lifestyle editors and journalists as well as reporters who cover community events. The CAGA spokesperson that you will quote in the release is Johnny McDonald, president of CAGA.

Case Study B

Henri Blanc has hired your public relations agency to promote an event in Toronto to attract media attention and to create awareness about his new upscale French bistro in Yorkville, Chez Restaurant.

Background information: There are more restaurants per capita in the City of Toronto than in almost any other city in North America; competition among high-end restaurants is fierce. Chez Restaurant has a prime location, valet parking, and a cordon bleu chef, M. Boeuf. He was trained in Paris, France, where he worked for twenty years in five-star restaurants.

Your menu is world class, as is your décor. Your prices reflect your chef, menu and the dining experience, which is private, personal and exquisite. You expect to attract celebrities, CEO and deal-makers.

The idea: To invite selected media—business editors and restaurant reviewers—to a grand opening gala party featuring fine finger foods and wine tasting. Jazz singer and crooner Michael Barns would provide the entertainment. The event would include brief presentations by M. Blanc and M. Boeuf. The gala will be held the day before the opening of the Toronto International Film Festival; a number of movie stars, producers and directors have accepted invitations to the opening.

The invited media and guests will receive private invitations. The media release will announce the grand opening gala, complete with red carpet. The goal is to create buzz with a big splash outside the restaurant—fans and media lining the red carpet; lots of red carpet photo opportunities—while providing guests with an intimate and private experience inside the restaurant.

Your task: Outline your *W5* and write a release that will capture the attention and hold the interest of the media and your target market. Focus on including your entire *W5* in the lead and working the most important aspects of it into the headline and sub-head. Expand on the most important aspect of your *W5*, and introduce any new elements, in your quote paragraph and in other paragraphs in the release. Don't forget to add an "about" and a "contact" section at the end of the release. Finally, feel free to identify several publications (or sections of newspapers) as well as broadcast outlets and blogs that you might send the media release to. Or identify the types of publications, broadcast outlets and blogs you might send it to.

Write a media release, or at least an opening paragraph and headline/sub-head, for either case study before you continue to read.

14/ Writing Case Studies

Below, you will find a case study on why to add case studies to websites. It is structured in typical case study fashion. I say typical, but the fact is there are a number of ways you can structure case studies. As you might imagine, a lot has to do with the purpose of the case study. Business case studies generally start with a problem, outline a solution and list the benefits of the solution. They then end with some information about the company that offers the solutions, as well as contact information.

The problem generally is an industry-wide problem and the goal of most case studies is to make the problem feel real for any reader (target audience) in a particular industry.

How do we do that? With something similar to a poster child, of course. The poster child is a company with a problem that represents the many—all the other companies out there that have the same, or similar, problem, generally (but not always) in a defined sector. The poster child company, its problem and the solution it implemented is described in the case study.

The case study below is very generic and does not open with a poster child lead. It appears on my blog and is meant to help me sell my case study writing services; however, there is a case study in Appendix II that includes a poster child company—a company in a specific industry with a specific problem that other companies in that industry might have. Of course the case study also includes the solution implemented to solve the problem and information on the company that provided the solution.

Some case studies, like the one in Appendix II, have additional sections. Additional sections might include the process a company went through to find a solution, failures the company experienced before finding a solution, the benefits and unexpected benefits of the solution, where the company sees itself going now that the problem is solved. And there are case studies that include less information and perhaps even no additional sections. Nevertheless, if they are well written, you should be able to see, at minimum, the problem, the solution and the benefits.

Now here's where it gets a bit fuzzy.

I have written case studies for various publications, and have been paid by the publication for doing so. I have also written case studies for companies that have solutions to solve problems and have been paid by the company that offers the solution. The case studies that I have written for publications have appeared in the publications; the case studies that I have written for companies have appeared on the websites of companies. The fuzziness revolves around the editing and approval process. When I write for publications, the editor edits and approves the case study for publication. The companies in the case study have no say on the final edit. When I write for companies that are paying me, a representative of the company does the final edit and approves the case study for use by the company.

I don't want to go into detail on this, other than to say whoever has assigned the case study and is paying for the work generally has the final say on how you structure your work and on what you write.

With that in mind, read the case study below to find out more about case studies and how they are used. Following it, you will find information on the kind of thinking and outlining you will want to do before you write a case study.

The Case Study Case Study

The problem

You have a business. You solve problems for your clients. You help them take advantage of opportunities. Or you save them time and money. You are good at what you do. The question is this: How do you tell the world?

You set up a website, one that extols the virtues of the products or services you offer. You make sure your website content includes key words, the kind of words and phrases prospects would use when searching for the goods or services you offer. But somehow the content, no matter how well it is written, feels a tad self-promotional. It sits on the page extolling your virtues, as it should, but you wonder how you can make it feel less like advertising copy and more like a real life business solution.

Then one of your best clients calls. He needs more of what you offer. He extols your virtues, telling you how your product is helping his business run more effectively and efficiently, is solving problems, or is helping him take advantage of opportunities.

And it hits you: If you had his words on your website, your content would sparkle and inspire. It would feel real. You think about asking your client for a testimonial, as you should, but you wonder how you can capture all your client said, and all your product does, in three to five sentences.

The solution

You know the problem your client was facing. You know the difficulty he was having solving the problem (or taking advantage of the opportunity). You know what he tried, unsuccessfully, to do. You know why he came to you. You know what you sold him and you know exactly how it helped.

Armed with that information, and your client's permission, you can write a 300- to 750-word case study and post it on your website or in your company blog.

"We write and issue media releases for clients and help them communicate using social media. This can build a brand and drive sales. Importantly, it also drives traffic to websites. The fact is, prospects seldom buy before they visit a website," says Alan McLaren, co-CEO, Infinity Communications (www.infinity-pr.com), a full service communications agency specializing in public relations, branding and social media strategies. "Having several case studies on your website is one of the best ways to show your product in action and to showcase how you help clients solve problems or take advantage of business opportunities."

The benefits

There are several benefits to posting case studies on your website and in your blog. Case studies are more than content that describe your product or service; they are more than a few lines of client testimonial as well. By detailing specific problems that your product has solved, or opportunities that it was used to exploit, case studies show how your products or service helped a real company or organization in a real situation. In other words, they extol the benefits of working with you from the perspective of a third party and outline the benefits derived from the use of your product.

"Case studies should spell out the issue, describe the solution and detail the benefits of implementing the solution," says McLaren. "Without being overly promotional, and using concise, focused writing, case studies should position your company and its products or services as the solution your prospect is seeking."

In short, case studies are a great way to extol the benefits of the products or services that you offer because they add third party legitimacy. They also boost the search engine optimization (SEO) of your website by using keywords or phrases someone might type in when searching for the kind of products or services that you are offering.

If you don't have case studies on your website, you might want to think about posting several online so you can effectively promote your products and services to website visitors.

More information

If you want to reap the benefits of having rich content on your website, but don't have the time to write informative case studies, contact Paul Lima – info@paullima.com or (416) 628-6005. Or visit his website to read more about him – www.paullima.com.

Pre-Writing Work

As with writing any document, before you write a case study, there are a few things you need to know and a few things you should do.

First off, you want to know the target audience. Are the readers all in a particular sector, or can they be readers from multiple sectors? I am presuming they all have, or potentially have, the same problem, but it's worth double checking the sectors the primary readers represent.

There is some practical information you need to know about the case study that has nothing to do with the content per se, but has an impact on the content. For instance, how long should the case study be? If this can be determined by you, no problem. Usually, however, it is determined by a manager or client. I've written case studies from three hundred and fifty words to over a thousand words. Most of the case studies that I write tend to be two pages (with designed headlines and corporate logos) that are converted into PDF files. If asked to write a case study, the best thing you can do is ask for an approximate word count, just as you would ask an editor how many words long an article should be.

While the word length does not affect the content, it does effect how you structure and convey the content.

As mentioned in the media release chapter, when you are writing articles, the editor will generally write the headline and sub-head. If you are writing case studies, you will write any headlines and sub-heads for corporate clients. You might suggest them for publications, but the editor reserves the right to write the final headline and sub-head.

If there is a case study style that the company uses, then you would simply follow that style when writing the body of the case study—the number of sections and focus of each section, for example. If there is no corporate case study guide, then you would discuss this with the client before you started your research and writing. (When it comes to determining structure, the example above and the one in Appendix II are great places to start. In addition, there are countless examples of case studies on the web.)

Questions that Affect What You Write

As you know by now, or should if I've been communicating effectively, I am a proponent of "think before you write." Not only do I believe you should outline any document before you write it, but I believe you should ask certain questions to gather information before you outline a document. How to conduct extensive interviews and research goes beyond the scope of this book, but ensuring you have your *W5* outlined, at minimum, is a great place to start when it comes to gathering information.

With case studies, as with some other articles, there can be more than five Ws. As we have seen with media releases, there is often why the company is issuing a media release versus the why used in the release: what the company hopes to accomplish by issuing the release versus why the information in the release is news. With complex feature articles, there could be multiple *W5*s based on dissenting or contrary opinions and points of view.

Before you outline and write a case study, complete several *W5*s: one on the company with the problem, one on the solution, one on the company with the solution, one on how the solution was implemented, and one on the benefits of the solution. You might not have 5 *W*'s for each aspect of the case study, but you won't know that until you think it through.

Once you have your *W5*s above in place, you create your big picture outline: list the sections of your case study. They might be as follows:

- Company (with the problem)
- Problem
- Process (of searching for a solution)
- Solution
- Implementation of the solution
- Benefits of the solution
- Company (with the solution).

Once you have your big picture case study in place, use your *W5* to help you outline each section. You may need (probably will need) additional points in each section based on your research and interviews, but the *W5* is the place to start. Then add any additional points and put them in logical order. Presto! You have an outline. You can then write from point to point to point until you have completed your first draft.

Again, see Appendix II for the sample case study, but remember your case study may not follow the format described here or in the Appendix.. It is up to you, your marketing department or your client to determine the format you want to use.

15/ Social Media

At the risk of sounding like a broken record, when it comes to writing anything, including social media content—tweets, LinkedIn and Facebook posts, blog posts or other content—you want to know your purpose (why you are writing, what you hope to achieve), your target reader, the word count (or in some cases, such as Twitter, the character count), format you should follow and any call to action you might want to make.

You do your research, which could be internal, or external, outline your document keeping the above points in mind, and then you write.

"Even for a 140-character tweet?" I can hear you asking.

My answer, or I wouldn't be sounding like a broken record, is, as always, "Yes."

You might spend (definitely will spend, in most cases) less time on all of the above if you are tweeting, but answer me this: Would you write a tweet without knowing why you want to write it? Would you tweet—and here I am talking business, not just social "here's what I did today" stuff—without knowing who you were targeting and why? Would you produce those 140 characters (or less) without thinking about who you are or whom you represent and your relationship with your target reader? Would you send your tweet into cyberspace without knowing what, if anything you hoped the reader would do? (I am not saying you have to have a call to action in mind when you tweet; I am saying you should think about whether you want to include one or not.)

When you tweet, you want to think about all that. Otherwise, why are you tweeting? What are you trying to accomplish?

But more on what you want to say, and how you might say it, in a bit. First, some background information. And when we get to the end of the chapter on blogging, there will be an exercise to help you put social media theory into practice.

What is Social Media?

But I'm getting ahead of myself. Let's look at what social media is.

Social media content, often called user-generated content, includes websites such as LinkedIn, Facebook and blogs, as well as Twitter tweets and (to a lesser extent) online discussion forums. YouTube is also a social media site, a video-based site, that we will mention in passing. And there are many new and developing social media sites, such as Google+, Google's attempt to become the new Facebook, Pinterest, an online site where you can collect and organize things that inspire you, and many others.

This chapter includes an overview of social media in general and of LinkedIn, Facebook and Twitter specifically, with a passing glance at online discussion forums and YouTube. In the next chapter, we go blogging.

Social Media Stats

Social media has grown faster than any other media to date. For instance, it took radio thirty eight years to reach fifty million listeners. It took TV thirteen years to reach fifty million viewers. The Internet hit fifty million surfers in four years. Facebook hit two hundred million users in less than a year and has now surpassed one billion users. To put the growth of social media into context, social media has overtaken porn as the number one activity on the web, so you know there are many, many people engaged in social media.

Facebook

All of Facebook's users are on the Internet, but not all Internet users are on Facebook; however, Facebook users congregate in one place—on Facebook. Because so many people are on Facebook, advertisers want to be there too.

Facebook users tend to chat and interact socially, but the site is used for promotional purposes because it has so many subscribers. Companies run ads on Facebook and many companies have Facebook sites. In fact, some business-to-consumer companies often don't include their corporate website in ads; instead, they include their Facebook address (www.facebook.com/company-name) and try to drive Facebook members to their Facebook pages. They hope visitors will read their promotional messages and view videos, "like" their page, engage in discussion and post positive comments, enter contests, and interact in other ways the company initiates. In other words, they try to make their Facebook page "sticky"—to get visitors there, keep visitors there, and to keep them coming back.

When it comes to writing for Facebook, there are several things you can do, such as write Facebook ads, posts on your social site or posts on a company site. Ads and social sites are not part of this book, but we'll take a moment and look at posts on company sites.

Take the Dove Facebook page. Dove has one million Facebook fans. On its Facebook home page (www.facebook.com/dove), the company has copy, images and links to videos. While some of the material promotes products, some of it promotes causes that the company supports.

On its Facebook wall, Dove starts with an introduction (about the company). Now Dove is a huge company and it could probably fill a page talking about itself. But would readers read a long missive on Dove? Probably not. Here is what Dove has on its wall:

Dove is committed to helping all women realize their personal beauty potential by creating products that deliver real care. Visit www.dove.ca for more information.

Short and sweet, no? Notice that it is not selling, at least not overtly, and that its target market—women—is clearly identified. Also notice that if you want to read a whole lot more about Dove, there is a link to its website. So while there is no hard-sell call to action, the reader can take action if she wants to know more. In this way, Dove extends the life of its Facebook introduction—for those who want more.

I happen to be writing this information about Dove on International Women's Day (IWD). Who is Dove's target audience? Women. That we know. So it's no surprise that Dove has information on its Facebook page today that pertains to IWD:

Want to do something to celebrate International Women's Day? Join us and help women around the world feel more beautiful by taking over negative ads! http://on.fb.me/ZlqmJq

Again, short and sweet. The content reinforces Dove's brand and position in the market as a company that is committed to creating a positive image for women. In short, notice how the IWD blurb relates directly to the content and tone of the opening blurb on the page. This is called focusing on a message. The link at the end of the IWD blurb extends the message, for those interested in knowing more.

Here is part of Dove's Facebook mission statement:

Dove on Facebook is about promoting positive self-esteem and helping women feel good about their unique inner and outer beauty....

Is it fair to say that, over these three posts, we have a theme and we are sticking to it? So even when you are writing short, you might be writing a lot and you want to know who you are writing for, what you want to say and why, and any action you want the reader to take. And you then want to focus on and repeat your theme to the extent it makes sense to the reader.

Finally, on its Facebook wall, where interactive dialogues take place, Dove initiates the discussion with posts like this:

Do you have sensitive skin? Has your Dermatologist or Doctor ever recommended using Dove Sensitive Skin?

Visitors can "like" the message or respond to it, such as this reply from Alicia:

I've been devoted to Dove for over 30 years. WON'T use anything else. The sensitive skin product is awesome! Thanks.

While there is room for a writer to produce Facebook promotions, user-generated comments represent terrific word-of-mouth and they are important: 78% of social media users trust peer reviews; 14% of TV watchers trust ads. So sometimes the goal of the writer is to write posts that generate positive comments on social media sites. And yes, some companies cheat. They have been accused of planting positive comments on various social media sites. If that trend continues, trust will diminish. While companies that use social media need to drive their agenda, they don't want to cause people to feel that they are being manipulated—or the social media network will call companies out and generate negative publicity.

LinkedIn

LinkedIn is the world's largest business-to-business (and professional-to-professional) social media network, with over one hundred million members and growing. LinkedIn members do things such as:

- Connect with contacts in their industry
- Boost brand awareness
- Showcase their knowledge by exchanging ideas, insights and opportunities with professionals in their target market

On LinkedIn, you can set up a company profile and personal profiles for employees who join the site. Individual and corporate profiles on LinkedIn should be professionally written and reflect any key messages a company wants to convey about itself and its products, services and support. In other words, when writing profiles for LinkedIn you want to follow the writing process so that your writing is a concise and focused and targeted as possible.

Many people join LinkedIn, connect with others or accept invitations to connect, and then do nothing. One way, however, to raise a personal or corporate profile, and build brand awareness, is to participate in discussion groups. While finding and joining various discussion groups goes beyond the scope of this book, I will say that LinkedIn makes it easy to do. The key, once you join (or start) a group, is to participate in an open manner that is not overtly promotional.

As a discussion forum group member you can post relevant questions, answer questions posted by others or comment on answers others give. Posting questions about issues or problems can be a good way to get discussions going. At the same time, answering questions can be an excellent way to demonstrate your knowledge about issues and situations. Most groups are moderated, which is good because it minimizes spam posts and ensures a degree of decorum.

Participating on discussion boards, where your target market might hang out discussing industry-related issues, involves writing. And before one posts to a discussion forum on behalf of the company they work for, they should know what impression they want to make and how to best make it—from the perspective of the reader, not the writer. If an issue is particularly important, the person posting a response might want to get a copywriter or editor to review and edit a message before it is posted.

If I work in your sector and I post a question pertaining to a sector problem, issue or opportunity, do I want you to blow your horn about how great your products and services are, or do I want you to offer concrete and useful information? I presume you'd say the latter. And if I offer concrete and useful information—well-written and logically structured replies—you just might, at some point down the road, investigate my products or services. How will you know where to find me? In the signature that I end my post with, of course.

I don't try to sell myself when I participate in business-related discussion forums. But if anyone is interested in contacting me or visiting my website, they don't have to look far, because all the information they'd need is in my signature:

Regards,
Paul Lima
Freelance Writer and
Business Writing Trainer
Ph.: (416) 628-6005
E: writer@paullima.com
Web: www.paullima.com

Companies can advertise on LinkedIn, as they can on Facebook. If they chose to do so, all the principles addressed in this book and my advertising copywriting book, *Copywriting that Works*, come into play. Ads on LinkedIn, which are similar to ads on Facebook, Google and other search engines, should capture the attention of a defined target market and motivate people to click. When ads are clicked on, they should lead to an online landing page, not a corporate home page. The landing page should encourage visitors to take a specific action—be it buy, donate, ask for a sales representative to call, complete a survey, support a cause, sign a petition, and so on.

Twitter

Twitter has been defined as the social media networking site for those who do not have many real friends and require random strangers to know minute details of their daily lives. However, Twitter is not used solely for short (maximum 140 characters) personal comments. People comment on all sorts of topics—personal life, social situations, causes and issues, politics, celebrity gossip, products and services, and so on.

Twitter has well over one hundred million users, although many subscribers seldom tweet and don't regularly read tweets of those people they follow, or they tweet a lot when they join and then the novelty wears off.

If you tweet, as posting a message on Twitter is called, nobody receives what you have to say unless they choose to follow you. How to gain Twitter followers goes beyond the scope of this book but allow me to quickly point out one way: look for and follow people who tweet about topics of interest to you or your company. The people you follow can then choose to follow you. You can also follow the followers of the person you chose to follow. Again, they may choose to follow you back. (There are other ways to build your followers; a quick Google search on the topic will reveal a number of articles that may be of interest.)

So do I tweet?

Absolutely. I use Twitter to help sell my books and my writing and training services. You might be able to easily imagine promotional tweets that I might write, but my followers don't really want to read promotions about Paul Lima. Hence, I blog as well, and then use tweets to drive people to practical information on my blog (see Circle of Social Media below). Here are a couple of tweet examples:

The anatomy of writing a speech or presentation - http://fb.me/IrRpKh42

5 Questions to ask before you start to write your non-fiction book - http://ow.ly/jlys8

Introduction to "Unblock Writer's Block" now online - http://ow.ly/jlyf8

The Case Study case study: A case study on why to add case studies to your website: http://ow.ly/jjNZO

And I even tweet testimonials for my work, as in this example:

"Excellent exercises for overcoming writer's block. Don't sit down without it!" – Tony Levelle, freelance writer - http://ow.ly/jm7wK

That does not mean you have to blog in order to tweet. It means you have to have something worth saying; something that your Twitter connections want to read and will find useful, interesting and/or entertaining.

With that in mind, should companies join Twitter? There is only so much companies can do but if a company feels its target market is on Twitter, then it should consider tweeting. Companies can use Twitter to build brand awareness by tweeting about existing and new products and services. They can also use tweets to drive traffic to their websites, Facebook pages and blogs (see circle of social media below).

Anatomy of a Tweet

When it comes to the anatomy of a tweet, there is no one tweet style fits all. Again, by way of broken record, what you tweet depends (at minimum) on your purpose, target reader and any action you want the reader to take—all in no more than 140 characters.

Companies have studied the components of effective tweets and have found some common denominators that you will want to keep in mind when tweeting.

Include links: tweets that included links were three times more prevalent in retweets than those without

Opt for timely news when possible: tweets mentioning timely news or events were the most shared. It may not always be possible (it may even seldom be possible) to share news. But there is good news beyond news, the most shared tweets were instructional in nature (followed by entertainment, opinion, products and small talk).

Share tech news (or maybe mention a celebrity): Again, this won't apply to everyone, but researchers at UCLA said tweets about tech news were the most shared. Health news and "fun stuff" were number two and three in terms of popularity.

Use hash tags in your tweets: If you are tweeting about something timely, or if you are tweeting about something that others who may not be following you could be interested in, use hash tags (the # symbol) beside key words in your tweets. For instance, when I tweet about writing or the business of freelance writing, I hash tag words like #writing and #freelance. My daughter works as a writer on a web series, Versus Valerie, and when people who promote the series tweet about it, they use the hash tag #VersusValerie. Hash tags make it easy for people interested in the topic to search for and find tweets on the subject.

Use "you" instead of "I": Among the words most commonly found in heavily shared tweets are "you," "Twitter," "please," "retweet," "post" and "check out." **Note:** asking someone to "please retweet" is a bit of a tacky practice you might want to avoid.

Circle of Social Media

Positive cyber word of mouth can help spread your message and drive traffic to a website using what I call "the circle of social media."

For instance, a company can announce a contest on its website and/or in its blog. It can then use Facebook, LinkedIn, Twitter and other social media to promote the contest. In its promotions it would, of course, include a link to the contest page on its website or blog. That would drive traffic to the contest. Also, if the company tweets about the contest and its followers retweet the tweet, more people will get to read about the contest and click through for details.

Companies can use the circle of social media, as can individuals.

As you know, I am a freelance writer, author and writing trainer. While my website, www.paullima.com, reflects that, my blog, www.paullima.com/blog, on the other hand is primarily (not exclusively) used to promote my books on copywriting, business writing and the business of freelance writing. When I create a new blog post, I post the title of the post and its website address on my Facebook page, on LinkedIn and on Twitter. That helps drive traffic to my blog post, which contains links to where people can purchase my books (if so inspired by my blog post), and the circle of social media is complete.

My hope is that the informative blog post will raise my profile and make me seem like a credible author, as well as spur people to like and repeat my messages. That, I hope, will drive additional traffic to my blog and help spur the sale of my books.

In addition, my blog (as with most blogs) has links to my LinkedIn, Twitter and Facebook accounts so people can choose to follow me on those media.

YouTube and Other Social Media

Most **YouTube** users create and post funny, odd or quirky videos on YouTube, or post social commentaries on a variety of topics; however, many companies and individuals, such as musicians and authors, post promotional videos on the site.

Once a video has been posted on YouTube, it can be embedded in a website or blog or on Facebook, and linked to LinkedIn and Twitter. Again, the goal is to use social media (writing) to drive viewers to the promotional video and to create buzz about it.

While Lady Gaga (or her recording company) can post a Lady Gaga music video on YouTube and have over a million people view it in a matter of days, companies should not expect to reach a mass audience. And why would they want to? For the most part, companies want to reach their target market. If a video is well made (well written and well produced) and contains valuable and/or informative information, it can attract an appropriate viewership— members of the identified target market. And if viewers like it, they can embed it in blogs and on Facebook and post links to it on LinkedIn and Twitter. So YouTube can be a viable promotion vehicle.

There are many other social media sites, too many to list here. But here are several that might be of interest to companies.

Tumblr is a site that lets you share anything—text, photos, quotes, links, music and videos—from your browser, phone, desktop, email, or wherever you happen to be.

Flickr is an online photo management and sharing application. The site has two main goals: to help people make their photos available to a select or mass audience, and to enable new ways of organizing photos and video. Companies can use Flickr but, as with any marketing, they should have a concrete business reason—building brand or product awareness, raising profile, driving sales—before choosing to use the site.

Google+ is a social networking and messaging tool from Google, designed to integrate into the company's web-based email program, Gmail. Users can share links, photos, videos, status messages and comments organized in "conversations" and visible in the user's inbox. (Since this book was first published, Google has abandoned "Buzz" and now runs **Google+** as its social media site.)

There is a list of social media sites, and what they are about, on Wikipedia – http://en.wikipedia.org/wiki/List_of_social_networking_websites.

Wikipedia itself is a social media site, in that users generate the content on the site. In other words, companies can have Wikipedia entries on the site— entries that can be edited by anyone who has a Wikipedia account. And if people feel a Wikipedia entry is incorrect or offensive (and incorrect or offensive is in the eye of the beholder) they will alter the post.

Follow Paul on...

If you are interested in seeing how I use social media, you can connect with me in various places:

- Twitter – https://twitter.com/PaulWriterLima
- Facebook – www.facebook.com/paul.lima
- "Like" my Facebook fan page – www.facebook.com/pages/Paul-Lima/183948319355?ref=nf
- Subscribe to my blog – www.paullima.com/blog
- LinkedIn - www.linkedin.com/profile/view?id=4128829&trk=tab_pro
- View my *How To Write A Non-Fiction Book In 60 Days* YouTube trailer – www.youtube.com/watch?v=ytmUI17gtgg

16/ Writing Blog Posts

Blogs are an online phenomena, with well over five hundred million blogs, and growing, out there. (Even though, it must be added, many are "ghost blogs"—blogs that have been abandoned in cyberspace.) And yes, many blogs are frivolous and personal; indeed, some companies think blogs are only used by people who are interested in celebrity gossip or venting about some perceived injustice.

In other words, there is a feeling that blogs are not used for business purposes. However, when it comes to blogging, you don't have to care what individuals are posting in their blogs. All you have to care about is *your* content.

Blogs that present solid business, technical or related-industry information are read on a regular basis. Company blogs may not attract a mass consumer readership, but that is not the goal of such blogs. As with other promotions, blogs should be set up to attract the attention of a defined target market, not a fractured mass audience.

Note: If you want to see how I use the content in this chapter on my blog to promote my freelance writing services—in this instance, my freelance blog-writing services—without going hard sell, visit my *Why Blog* index page on my blog: http://paullima.com/blog/?cat=397.

There are many reasons why companies should blog and take a planned, systematic approach to producing useful, informative and compelling blog content that focuses on topics of interest to their target market. Blogs can, for instance, boost the rank of a company's website in search engine results, help companies deepen their relationship with existing customers, engage new prospects and build their brand in the online universe.

Imagine Your Target Market Seeking You

Imagine spending nothing but a bit of time to create compelling content about your company, your products and services, or trends and issues pertaining to your industry, and having people in your target market actively seeking out and reading this content.

That is what blogs enable you to do. And that is marketing heaven.

Ironically, however, many companies do not blog, blog erratically or only post blatantly promotional notices in their blog. In short, they miss this simple, low-cost and effective marketing opportunity.

To attract and hold readers, your blog posts must be interesting, informative and credible. You have to give your readers something they want to read, because it helps them learn something important, work more effectively or productively, or helps them solve problems, save time or money, discover new opportunities or take advantage of existing opportunities.

Also, to hold the interest of your audience, you need to blog on a regular basis. Regular blogging does not mean daily, as too much information can overwhelm readers. Blogging once a week seems to work for many companies, although some companies blog several times a week or a couple of times a month.

Keep Content Short(ish)

When blogging, you want to make sure your blog posts are not too long, otherwise they will not be read all the way through. Length is relative based on the topic being addressed; however, effective blog posts tend to run two hundred to six hundred words in length. That does not mean they can't be longer on occasion, but they should not be much longer on a consistent basis. Or, on the other hand, if you have something lengthy to say, you can post a synopsis of the topic on your blog and link from your blog post to a web page or PDF. The most interested readers will click on the link (you should be able to measure click-throughs) and continue to read.

Build Relationships

Blogs can help business-to-business (B2B) and business-to-consumer (B2C) companies deepen their relationship with existing customers. People who buy products from companies, especially if they are complex ones, like to have their purchase reinforced. In other words, even after they buy, they like to read good news about the product—how it works and can be used.

This kind of information helps reinforce their purchase decision. With their purchase decision reinforced, they are more likely to become repeat customers and more likely to tell others about their purchase. And, as most companies know, no marketing is more cost-effective than repeat business and no marketing is more effective than positive word of mouth.

Driving traffic to a company blog can raise the credibility of the company and boost its online brand awareness. But this doesn't amount to anything unless the company can close the sale. That is why companies include links on their blogs to specific product and contact pages.

Just as every prospect who reads ads about a company's products will not buy, not every blog reader will click on links to the company's website, but the links are there for readers who want to know more. And knowing more is the first step prospects take before they buy.

Generating Blog Post Topics

Before you write a blog post, clearly decide on your topic, which segment of your target market the post will appeal to, and what problem or opportunity you will address. Your post should stay focused on that topic, segment and issue. This might mean some prospects will not be interested in particular posts; however, if you try to be everything to everybody in each post, you will end up being nothing to nobody.

With that in mind, create some big-picture subject areas that you can blog about, including industry trends, issues and opportunities, and specific issues and opportunities for various sectors of your target audience. Use clustering to help you come up with big picture topics. Once you have your big picture ideas, brainstorm blog-post ideas or topics under each big-picture subject. Within an hour or two, you can develop a number of blog post topics—topics that will be of interest to various segments of your target market.

Once you have developed the topics, create a schedule—a list of topics, the dates you will blog about each topic, and who within your company (or outside your company, such as industry analysts or customers) will write the blog posts. And make sure any post is well edited before it goes online.

Your blog post schedule will keep you on track so that your blog has a constant flow of new and compelling content, which will help hook readers and keep them coming back. Of course, as industry issues emerge, or if you produce new products/services or revamp existing ones, you can revise the schedule and make room to cover emerging issues or to blog about your new products or product updates. Beware, however, of making your blog content overly promotional.

While you can produce solid, simple and factual descriptions about your products, I suggest you go beyond such posts and blog about industry trends and issues (this is where brainstorming topics come into play) to demonstrate the extent to which you understand your industry. You can, of course, relate some of these issues to your products, but you don't always have to do that. Sometimes simply demonstrating an understanding of an issue or opportunity, without overt commercial overtones, helps build your standing in the industry.

How to Write Blog Posts

Blog posts generally have three sections—introduction, body and conclusion.

Introductory paragraph: The crucial part of any blog post is the introductory paragraph. It should be no more than a couple of lines and should summarize what the post is about, i.e. after reading the first few lines, readers should know what the purpose of the post is and what they will learn or discover. That will entice readers to read on.

Body: Next comes the body of the post. Different points should always be separated by paragraphs and major topic shifts should have their own sub-heads, as we have in this post. The sub-head, in conjunction with the first sentence of each paragraph or section, should spell out the topic of the paragraph or section and lure readers into continuing to read.

Because readers scan or browse when they read online content, you'll want to keep your paragraphs short to avoid large, intimidating chunks of text. If it makes sense, add graphics to illustrate points, but don't add frivolous graphics for the sake of having images in your post.

If you want to convey a series of points, consider using bulleted or numbered lists (as in the Before You Write section of this post) because they are easier to scan and absorb than full paragraphs.

Conclusion: Finally, end your blog post with a conclusion or summary paragraph, a round-up of what you've been writing about. Or, if you've been making a case for the reader to take action, end with a call to action, a list of recommendations or a link to a follow-up web page.

Blog Headlines: Accurately Reflect Content

When creating a headline or title for your blog post, you don't need to be too creative. In fact, the more direct you are, the better the headline will be. For instance, "What happens when we drain Canada dry?" might make for a cute and effective newspaper headline, one that will cause curious readers to read the article when they stumble upon the headline. But it makes for a lousy blog headline for an article pertaining to the ecological consequences of diminishing water resources in Canada.

In other words, you want your blog headline to accurately reflect the content of your article. When your article is picked up by search engines, they will serve up your headline as the link to the blog post based on key words used for searches. How many people would search for "What happens when we drain Canada dry?" If somebody included "Canada Dry" in a search, they would most likely be looking for information on the soda pop by the same name. People interested in environmental issues might, however, search for "ecological consequences" or "diminishing water resources" and cause the search engine to serve up a link to your aptly titled article.

So don't try to write cute blog headlines; write headlines that accurately reflect the content of your blog post.

Or combine a practical approach with something cute, using your friend, the semi-colon, as in the following:

- What happens when we drain Canada dry: the ecological consequences of diminishing water resources
- How to write an effective blog headline: sexy doesn't always cut it
- Gotcha: How using W5 headlines and leads captures attention of readers

I think you get the point. Be practical. Doesn't mean you can't have any fun, but make sure you are also practical—if you want people to find your blog post using search engines. If you are driving hordes of traffic to your site using other means, be as sexy crazy as you want to be.

Putting Social Media Theory into Practice

By way of quick review, we've looked at Facebook, LinkedIn, Twitter, blogging and the circle of social media. Now it's time to put into practice the theory you've been reading about.

I could give you a series of exercises, but ideally the social media exercise you do should be based on your interests, be it the products or services you sell, the causes you support, or the products and services the company you work for sells.

With that in mind, I want you to engage in the circle of social media. You will write a blog post and try to drive traffic to it. Before you write, I want you to do a few things:

- Pick a product, service, cause, company, issue you'd like to write about.
- Jot down who you are in relation to the above (you might be a business owner, an employee, an interested third party and so on).
- Briefly describe your target reader, based on demographics (age, gender, income and so on), lifestyle, sector the reader works in, position within a company, type and size of company, and so on.
- In one sentence (that may be longer than a tweet), describe your writing purpose.
- Describe any action you hope a reader might take.
- Jot down a key word or phrase related to product, service, cause, company, issue you'd like to write about.
- Cluster that word or phrase.

Once you have completed the above process, here's what you do:

- Write a blog post on the issue (two hundred to five hundred words should do). Should your blog post include links to any websites? If so, make sure you include them. Also, make sure you give your blog post a title.

- Write three tweets related to the above blog post. One can simply be the title of the post. Make sure you include your blog post address. (Feel free to make one up if you don't actually have a blog.) Remember, the address is part of your 140 tweet characters. If your address is long, you can shorten it here: http://tinyurl.com/. **Note:** some tweet applications, such as HootSuite and TweetDeck automatically shorten website addresses.

- Write a short blurb, a summary as it were, of your blog post for Facebook and LinkedIn. Keep it to no more than fifty or so words and include your blog post address.

And you are done.

The next two chapters are on constructing sentences and paragraphs and transitions. They are followed by the Appendixes. And then, that's it folks.

I hope you've found the book informative and useful—something you can use to help make you a stronger, more polished writer, one who can craft concise, targeted, focused documents.

If you have any questions, or want to inquire about any of my other books, my writing or training services, please visit my website, www.paullima.com, or email info@paullima.com.

All the best with your writing.

17/ Constructing Sentences

In the beginning was the word. It was quickly followed by the sentence. Which, of course, was followed by the paragraph.

Do you know what the shortest sentence in the Bible is? Two words: *Jesus wept.* The sentence has a subject (*Jesus*) and a verb (*wept*). In theory, that is all a sentence needs to be complete.

Where, however, is the subject in the following two-word sentence?

Do it!

The subject, *you,* in a command or imperative is understood. Everyone who hears the simple command *Do it!* understands it to mean <u>You</u> do it. Drop the *you,* start the sentence with the verb (to do), and the sentence packs a more powerful punch.

Without a subject (real or implied) and verb, you have a sentence fragment:

Because I.
Over there.
The officer.

However, look at the third sentence in this chapter:

Which, of course, was followed by the paragraph.

When you read it, did you notice that it was a sentence fragment? (Where is the subject?) Did it feel like a fragment when you read it? Even if it did, was it effective? Does it feel like a fragment now that you are reading it out of context?

Although sentence fragments can be used effectively, particularly in fiction and advertising, seldom will you use them in business writing. If they are not used appropriately—for a conscious effect or to emphasize a particular point—they can create disjointed writing and can cause miscommunication and confusion.

Part of your goal as a business writer is to become aware of, and correct, sentence faults and other problems that can interfere with clear, concise communication. You do this when editing your work. In other words, don't get hung up on fixing them as you write. That will thwart your writing efficiency. At the same time, if you follow the writing process, especially the creation of detailed outlines, you will bring greater clarity to your writing—and so have fewer revisions to make when editing.

While grammar and spelling count, this is not a book about grammar and spelling. This is a writing and writing-process book. With that in mind, I will not spend time on sentence faults. We will, however, look again at active and passive voice and at examples of how to construct effective sentences.

Active Versus Passive Voice

Read the two passages below. What is different about them? What is similar?

The Highway Department is building a new bridge in River Hollow. The backhoe digs deep holes. The cement mixer pours in concrete to make the supports.

Carefully Carlton picks up steel girders with his crane and lays them across the supports.

Bulldozers push up the surrounding ground to make a road. The grading machine smoothes the slope, and the asphalt spreader pours down a layer of blacktop. Brian's steamroller comes last to smooth it flat and even. Dennis and Darlene haul away the extra dirt in their dump truck.

* * *

Research into new advertising promotions that could boost company sales was initiated by marketing last spring.

A list of primary media read by our Target Market was compiled by Susan McMillan. Creative ideas were produced by the copywriting department. A campaign was designed by Frank Myers, the art director, and was launched in the summer.

Encouraging have been the sales results to date.

Does the first passage remind you of a grade one reader? If you are old enough to have gone on adventures with Dick and Jane, it might remind you of those famous sentences that you read when you were first learning to read:

See Dick. See Jane. See Dick run. See Jane run. See Spot. See Spot run. Hear Spot bark.

The sentences above are clear and concise. But are they effective? Or are they boring and monotonous? Could you imagine reading an entire report with sentences written only like the ones in the first or the second passage above?

In the first passage, the simple sentences are written in the active voice, which can be used to create short, direct sentences. The second passage is written entirely in the passive voice, which makes for longer, more awkward sentences that distance the reader from who did what.

While the most effective sentences are generally written in the active voice, effective writing requires variety—a mix of active and passive voice, a mix of complex and simple sentences, and the use of sentences of various lengths.

Active Voice

We are not going to get bogged down in grammatical terms; however, I need to use two: *subject* and **verb**. In the active voice, the *subject* performs the action expressed in the **verb**. In other words, the subject acts, as in the examples below:

The dog **bit** the boy.

Terri **will present** her research at the conference.

We **received** your shipment two days late, which caused delays.

You **sent** the shipment two days late, which caused delays.

Scientists **have conducted** experiments to test the hypothesis.

Passive Voice

In sentences written in the passive voice, the *subject* receives the action expressed by the **verb**. The agent performing the action may appear in a "by the..." phrase or may be omitted entirely.

The boy **was bitten** by the dog.

Research **will be presented** by Terri at the conference.

Your payment **was received** two days late, which caused delays.

Experiments **have been conducted** to test the hypothesis.

Notice the agents committing the action are missing from the last two sentenced. Here are the last two sentences with the "by the" agents included:

Your payment was received two days late by the accounting department, which caused delays.

Experiments have been conducted by the scientists to test the hypothesis.

Do you need "by the accounting department" or "by the scientists" in the above sentences? The sentences are grammatically correct without the agents. If, however, it was important for the reader to know that the accounting department did not receive the payments, or that scientists conducted the experiments, then the agents should be included. If not, no problem leaving the agents out.

Leaving the scientists out of the second sentence puts the focus on the experiments and why they were conducted. There is nothing wrong with this focus, if that is where you want to put it. In other words, where you put your emphasis or focus, and the voice you use, should be conscious decisions.

Having said that, you should know that the passive voice can create awkward sentences and cause readers to become confused. Sentences written in the active voice require fewer words than those written in the passive voice. This makes for writing that is more concise. In addition, sentences in the active voice are generally clearer and more direct than those in the passive voice.

The passive voice can allow writers to compose without using personal pronouns or names of people or groups (as with the scientists and accounting department sentences).This can help create the appearance of an objective, fact-based discourse. But the passive voice can also be used to deflect blame or avoid responsibility, which is not always warranted, as in the following sentence:

Seeking to lay off workers without taking the blame, consultants were hired to break the bad news.

Who was seeking to lay off workers? The consultants? That's what it looks like in this sentence. However, the CEO was more likely responsible. If that is the case, leaving out the agent creates a misleading sentence that avoids allocating proper responsibility. So let's use active voice and include the responsible party:

Seeking to lay off workers without taking the blame, the CEO hired consultants to break the bad news.

Being direct can be an important aspect of writing. On the other hand, there are times when being indirect is preferable. If there is no clear agent, then there is no clear blame, and sometimes it is necessary to point out a problem without pointing fingers, as in these examples:

Several mistakes were made before the trains collided.

The quota was not met last month, so monthly bonuses have been withheld.

In the quota example: The person making the announcement might know which person or department did not meet the quota, but has chosen not to say it publicly. Also, notice that the person making the announcement has not credited an individual—the CEO or a specific manager—for withholding bonuses. What we have here is the withholding of two agents and the double use of passive voice in one sentence, but it is not necessarily doublespeak. You might call it politically sensitive communication.

If we wanted to state who did not meet quota and who withheld the bonuses, here's what we might write (in active voice):

The CFO withheld bonuses because the Western Sales Team did not meet its quota last month.

In the train example: Imagine that a train collision is under review. It is obvious that the trains should not have collided. The spokesperson for the railway company cannot deny that a collision has occurred, because it obviously has. However, the spokesperson cannot say who made mistakes that caused the collision until the accident review is completed. Instead, she resorts to the passive voice and leaves out the agent so she does not allocate blame.

If she wanted to allocate blame, she could have written (or said) the following:

Several mistakes were made by the eastbound engineer before the trains collided.

And if she had used the active voice, she might have said this:

The eastbound engineer made several mistakes before the trains collided.

Choosing the Passive Voice

As mentioned, the passive voice highlights what is acted upon rather than focusing on the agent performing the action. It makes sense when the agent performing the action is obvious, unknown or unimportant. It also makes sense when a writer wishes to postpone mentioning the agent until the last part of the sentence, or to avoid mentioning the agent at all.

In the examples below, the passive voice makes sense if the agent is less important than the action and what is acted upon.

Active: The dispatcher notified police only minutes after three prisoners had escaped.

Passive: Police were notified only minutes after three prisoners had escaped.

If it is more important to know how long it took for the police to be notified than it is to know who notified the police, the passive voice makes sense. If there was some question as to who notified the police, and if that was more important than how long it took for the police to be notified, the active voice would make sense.

In the next sentence, what is more important: the spruce budworm or the irrevocable damage?

Active: The spruce budworm has irrevocably damaged vast expanses of Cape Breton forests.

Passive: Vast expanses of Cape Breton forests have been irrevocably damaged by the spruce budworm.

In the passive voice sentence, the emphasis is on the damage to the forests, not the cause of the damage. If, however, you wanted to warn people about the spruce budworm, the active voice would make more sense.

When choosing between the active and passive voice, keep the reader, your topic and your purpose in mind. Also, think about clarity and conciseness. In other words, make conscious decisions concerning the use of the active and passive voice. But beware of using the passive voice to mask issues that should be actively addressed.

Convert Passive to Active

Take a moment and convert the passive voice sentences below to active voice. If you are not sure that you have done it correctly, set grammar checker to flag passive constructions and grammar check your revised sentences. You can also look at the revised sentences at the end of this chapter.

The entrance exam was failed by more than one third of the applicants to the school.

The brakes were slammed on by her as the car sped downhill.

Your bicycle has been damaged.

(The agent has been omitted. Who did the damage? Edit the sentence as if you did and edit it as if a thief has damaged the bicycle.)

Action on the bill is being considered by the committee.

By then, the soundtrack will have been completely remixed by the sound engineers.

To satisfy the instructor's demands for legibility, the paper was written on a computer.

(Before revising this, ask who was satisfying the instructor? The paper? Or the person writing the paper? Then edit the sentence.)

Once you have converted the passive sentences to active voice, continue to read.

How to Construct a Sentence

As I mentioned, this is not a grammar book. I want to take a moment, however, to review the foundation of the sentence. At minimum, the sentence requires a subject and a verb (action). In *I laughed*, *I* is the subject; *laughed* is the verb. But two-word sentences generally don't cut it in business writing. So let's review a sentence that includes a *subject*, a **verb**, and a third component—the object.

The boy kicked the soccer ball.

The boy is our subject (the person who does the action). **Kicked** is the verb or action. The soccer ball is our object, that which receives the action. I call these three elements "the heart of the sentence." If you ever feel that your sentences are getting too complex, find the heart. Once you have the heart, you can expand your sentence logically and keep the meaning clear. For instance, where did the ball go when the boy kicked it?

The boy kicked the soccer ball through the window.

What happened to the window?

The boy kicked the soccer ball through the window, which shattered into a thousand pieces.

Tell me more about this boy:

The tall, thin, Caucasian boy kicked the soccer ball through the window, which shattered into a thousand pieces.

Do you see how our sentence is becoming more complex? It is easy to understand, however, because we can still identify the heart of the sentence. Now imagine that this action was committed by a criminal.

The tall, thin, armed and dangerous Caucasian boy kicked the soccer ball through the window, which shattered into a thousand pieces.

Notice how the above sentence is getting a tad long and awkward—a run-on sentence, as it were. Yet it is simpler than, and short than, many sentences used in business writing, so let's stick with it for a moment.

What happened next?

The tall, thin, armed and dangerous Caucasian boy kicked the soccer ball through the window, which shattered into a thousand pieces, and then he fled the scene.

Notice we now have two "hearts" combined. Let me simplify them for you:

The boy kicked the soccer ball through the window.
He fled the scene.

Two subjects, two verbs, two objects. One sentence. Meaning is still clear because we let one heart beat, so to speak, and then the other. So if you think sentences are running away on you, identify your subject and verb and build from there. If you have more than one subject and verb, identify each of them and determine how best to let them beat. Joined or as two separate sentences. If the complex sentence feels like it is unclear, separate the two hearts:

The tall, thin, armed and dangerous Caucasian boy kicked the soccer ball through the window, which shattered into a thousand pieces. Then he fled the scene.

Keep clear, concise, simple sentences in mind as you try the writing exercises in this book and as you write and edit your work.

Passive Voice Converted to Active Voice

The passive sentences presented earlier in this chapter have been converted to the active voice.

More than one third of the applicants to the school failed the entrance exam.
She slammed on the brakes as the car sped downhill.
I have damaged your bicycle.
The thief damaged your bicycle.
The committee is considering action on the bill.

By then, the sound engineers will have completely remixed the soundtrack.

I wrote the paper on a computer to satisfy the instructor's demands for legibility.

The student wrote the paper on a computer to satisfy the instructor's demands for legibility.

18/ Paragraphs and Transitions

A paragraph is a collection of sentences organized around a clearly defined topic. If you are writing a long document, each paragraph topic will be a subtopic of, or somehow related to, the subject of the document you are writing.

The paragraph performs three functions:

- Develops the unit of thought stated in the topic sentence
- Provides a logical break in the material
- Creates a visual break on the page, thus signalling a new topic

Generally, the paragraph starts with a topic sentence. Often, this topic sentence is an important outline point converted into a complete sentence. The topic sentence states the paragraph's main idea. The rest of the paragraph supports and develops the idea.

The topic sentence is often the first sentence in a paragraph because it tells the reader what the paragraph is about. However, the topic sentence can be used to end a paragraph—almost like a punch line. Occasionally, the topic sentence can be found in the middle of the paragraph. There would be some build up to the topic sentence, followed by the topic sentence, and then followed by some support of the topic.

Topic at the Beginning

Here is an example of writing with *the topic sentence* at the beginning of each paragraph:

The cost of orientation, health and safety, and customer service training for new Customer Service Representatives (CSRs) is significant. The organization must cover the price of classroom facilities, instructors and manuals and must pay employees their full salary, while they are non-productive, during the three-week training period.

If the company is to break even on its investment in training, employees must stay in the job for which they have been hired for at least one year, according to our analysis (see attached PDF). However, on average, customer service representatives leave the company within nine months of hiring. Not only is the company losing money on employee training, we are also paying exorbitant recruitment costs to fill each vacancy.

To increase the return on investment (ROI) for training new CSRs, the committee proposes that the following three recommendations be implemented within three months:

- Recommendation one ... .
- Recommendation two ... .
- Recommendation three ... .

Notice how the first sentence of the first paragraph establishes both the subject of the document as well as the topic of the paragraph: "The cost of... is significant." I suspect you could imagine this sentence being used to establish the topic about almost any paragraph dealing with cost issues, such as: *The cost of purchasing parts from our current supplier is significant.* In short, the sentence raises an issue, which creates expectations that the document will explain why the cost of whatever is significant and will most likely suggest how the issue can be resolved. The rest of the paragraph explains why the cost is significant and the document goes on to suggest how to solve the problem.

The opening sentence of the second paragraph does something interesting. It tells us the circumstances that must occur if we are to solve the problem and offers us proof. It does not, however, cram the proof into the document: "If the company is to break even on its investment in training, employees must stay in the job for which they have been hired for at least one year, according to our analysis (see attached PDF)."

It often makes sense to attach complex details to an email message or to include them in an appendix in a report. If readers believe you are addressing a valid issue, they will have no need to get bogged down in the details that prove it. By attaching the PDF, the writer can move quickly from the problem to the solution while offering skeptics proof in the attached document or report appendix.

Finally, notice how the third paragraph consists of a topic sentence and three points. (There will be more on when and why to use bullet points or numbered points later in this chapter.)

Topic at the End

Here is an example of writing with the topic sentence at the end of the paragraph:

Energy does more than simply make our lives more comfortable and convenient. If you wanted to reverse or stop economic progress, the surest way to do so would be to cut off the nation's oil resources. The country would plummet into the abyss of economic ruin. *In short, our economy is energy-based.*

Often—not always—opening paragraphs in email messages, letters, executive summaries of reports, and other documents place the topic sentence at the end of the paragraph. This lets the writer set the stage with a few lines that build up to the topic and purpose of the document.

Your topic and purpose can be made clear in the first line of the first paragraph, the last line of the first paragraph, or even part way through your first paragraph. The important thing is that, almost without exception, the reader needs to know what you are writing about (your topic) and why (your purpose) by the end of the opening paragraph. (There will be more on purpose later in the book.)

Paragraph Length

The length of each paragraph should aid the reader's understanding of the idea addressed. A series of very short paragraphs can indicate poor organization and underdeveloped thoughts. However, if they unfold in al logical order, they can be effective on the web. (But that is a whole other topic.) Too many long paragraphs can fail to provide the reader with manageable subdivisions of thought. The occasional one-sentence paragraph is acceptable if it is used for effect or as a transition between paragraphs. One-sentence paragraphs are also acceptable in short letters and memos—particularly as openings or closings.

Transitions

Transitions help the reader move smoothly from sentence to sentence and paragraph to paragraph. Think of transitions as a two-way indicator, pointing to what has been said and what will be said. In that way, transitions help readers link ideas and clarify the relationship between them. Conversely, a lack of transitions can make for disjointed reading. (*Conversely* is just one of many transitional words and phrases.)

Here are two examples of transitional sentences:

Having considered the costs and benefits of building a new facility, we move next to the question of adequate staffing.

Even if the new facility can be built at a reasonable cost, there is still the question of adequate staffing.

Transitions do not have to be so overt, nor do they have to be complete sentences. As we shall see, the transitional components of a sentence often appear at the beginning of a sentence; however, they can appear part way through the transitional sentence as well.

Transitions can be achieved by any of the following:

- Using transitional words or phrases between sentences
- Using transitional sentences between sentences or, more likely, between paragraphs
- Repeating key words or phrases that appear in one sentence in the next sentence
- Paraphrasing key words or phrases that appear in one sentence in the next sentence
- Numbering
- Summarizing a previous paragraph in a sentence between paragraphs.

Different transitional words or phrases have different functions. For example, *for example* is an excellent transition example. When a sentence begins with "for example," you expect to see the idea that preceded the transition made clear through use of an example or a case in point. In addition, when you see *in addition* at the beginning of a sentence, you expect the writer to add something to the idea or topic. However, when you see the word *however* in a sentence, you expect the information in the "however" sentence to contrast the information that has come before the sentence.

Transition words and phrases are often used at the beginning of sentences. You might, however, also see transition words used part way through a sentence, following the first clause, as *however* is used in this sentence.

The occasional however at the start of sentence is fine. However, if overused at the start of too many sentences in a passage, *however* can feel repetitive. That is one reason you might want to use *however* after the first clause of a sentence.

In fact, the esteemed grammarians Strunk and White in their book, *The Elements of Style*, suggest that one shouldn't start a sentence with however when one means "nevertheless" or "on the other hand." On the other hand, language evolves and modern usage of however when one means "nevertheless" or "on the other hand" has become more acceptable.

Transitions in Action

Do you remember Kevin Huber? With the above information in mind, read the article excerpt below and find the transition words, phrases, sentences, and so on in it.

Kevin Huber can navigate through his word processing package as fast as almost any other computer user. However, unlike most computer users, Kevin cannot see the keyboard or his monitor. In fact, other than differentiating between intense light and dark shadows, Kevin sees nothing.

Legally blind since birth, Kevin hears what others see thanks to adaptive technologies. Adaptive technologies are tools that translate visual information into audible information for visually challenged computer users.

Kevin has adjusted to his challenge so well that he now works as a client support representative for Microcomputer Science Centre in Mississauga, where he tests new computer technology intended for use by visually challenged persons. He also shows instructors how to train persons with disabilities to compute and surf the web using adaptive technology.

Like slanted sidewalks, or curb cuts, which are used to make streets more accessible to mobility challenged persons, adaptive technology, or electronic curb cuts, are used to make computers more accessible to physically challenged persons.

Physical challenges can be divided into three categories: visual, hearing, and mobility. Visual challenges range from reduced visual acuity to blindness. Hearing challenges range from slight loss of hearing to deafness. And mobility challenges range from impaired movement of limbs to limited movement of the head and lips.

The transitions are highlighted in a passage at the end of this chapter. However, try to find them before you move to the end of the chapter.

Once you have completed the transition exercise, continue to read.

Now that you are familiar with transitions, review your revised executive summary to see if you can find opportunities for weaving in transitions that will help the reader move more smoothly from point to point. If you can, edit your work again and apply smoother transitions. In addition, run your edited executive summary through your grammar checker. (Make sure your grammar checker is set to stop at passive voice.) If your grammar checker stops at a passive sentence, decide if you want to convert it to the active voice. Remember, passive voice is grammatically correct; however, you should consciously choose if you want a sentence to be in the active or the passive voice. In short, make informed, conscious decisions when editing.

Bullet and Numbered Points

As we saw previously in this chapter, in the topic sentence example about "the cost of orientation, health and safety, and customer service training," there are times when bullet point or numbered point sentences make sense.

Bullet and numbered points are easy to scan and absorb. They make sense when you are making a series of recommendations or when you are giving instructions—especially if the instructions must be performed sequentially. Look at the examples below. They are presented as conventional paragraphs and then as numbered points. Which ones make the most sense to you? Why?

Example I

For you to start juggling, you must do the following: first pick up A in your right hand, then you should pick up B in your left hand, and then you should toss A and then B into the air, catching A as you toss B and catching B and you toss A. Repeat continuously.

For you to start juggling, do the following:
1. Pick up A in your right hand.
2. Pick up B in your left hand.
3. Toss A into the air.
4. Toss B into the air while catching A.
5. Toss A back into the air while catching B.
6. Repeat continuously.

Example II

Three habits that improve health are getting eight hours of sleep each night, eating three balanced meals every day, and exercising regularly.

Three habits that improve health are

- Getting eight hours of sleep each night,
- Eating three balanced meals every day,
- Exercising regularly.

The numbered points convey the information in a manner that is easier to scan, absorb and understand. The shorter lines cause the eye to stop at the end of each point as the brain does a mental check. Then the eye moves to the beginning of the next point and repeats the pattern. With that in mind, look for opportunities to use bullet or numbered points. However, don't overdo it. A page full of bullet points can look almost as tedious to read as the wall-of-words executive summary presented earlier in this chapter. Also:

- Bullet points used for no reason don't make sense.
- If you use them just because you think you should, you could confuse the reader.
- The reader will be looking for a list of instructions or recommendations where no list exists.

In short, unnecessary and improper use of bullet points, as used above, don't advance the clarity of your writing and can even be confusing. Enough said, yes?

Transitions Highlighted in Italic

Kevin Huber can navigate through his word processing package as fast as almost any other computer user. *However,* unlike most computer users, Kevin cannot see the keyboard or his monitor. *In fact,* other than differentiating between intense light and dark shadows, Kevin sees nothing. *Legally blind* [illuminates *"sees nothing"*] since birth, Kevin hears what others see thanks to adaptive technologies. *Adaptive technologies* are tools that translate visual information into audible information for visually challenged computer users.

Kevin has adjusted to his *challenge* [links this paragraph to *"challenged"* in the previous paragraph] so well that he now works as a client support representative for Microcomputer Science Centre in Mississauga, where he tests new computer technology intended for use by visually challenged individuals. He *also* shows instructors how to train persons with disabilities to compute and surf the web using adaptive technology.

Like slanted sidewalks, or curb cuts, which are used to make streets more accessible to mobility challenged persons, adaptive technology, or electronic curb cuts, are used to make computers more accessible to physically challenged persons. [This is a transitional paragraph; we are leaving Kevin now to look at the actual technologies.]

Physical challenges can be divided into three categories: visual, hearing, and mobility. *Visual challenges* range from reduced visual acuity to blindness. *Hearing challenges* range from slight loss of hearing to deafness. And *mobility challenges* range from impaired movement of limbs to limited movement of the head and lips.

Appendix I: Full Articles

Article I

Headline: "There aren't even jobs to bag groceries" in Calgary

Cassandra Lees has found herself in a situation she would have thought impossible just a year ago – unemployed and unable to find work anywhere in Calgary.

When Lees, 28, moved to the city three years ago from Winnipeg, she couldn't walk down the street without seeing a "Help Wanted" sign in every retail window.

Employers were offering trips to new recruits and giving away cars as incentives to employees.

After months of looking for everything from secretarial work to part-time retail positions, Lees said she is painfully aware of a new reality.

"There aren't even jobs out there to stock shelves or bag groceries," she said.

No province is immune to declining fortunes, but Alberta's fall, after such dramatic highs as last summer's oil and gas prices, is steeper than anywhere else.

The province's economic activity is projected to fall by 2.3 percent this year, the sharpest drop among the provinces, according to an RBC report. Capital investments in the province have scaled back significantly, most noticeably in drilling for new wells.

Premier Ed Stelmach said Alberta has gone through recessions before when oil and gas prices fell but this time the provincial economy is better positioned to bounce back.

China and India are new customers that weren't developed during the last recession and low interest rates are good indicators that Alberta won't stay in a recession long, said Stelmach.

Stelmach said he knows it's tough right now for young people in their 20s who have never known a time when they couldn't find jobs.

"I tell young people that they should take the opportunity to upgrade your skills, the jobs will come back, no doubt about it," said Stelmach. "We go into a recession and come out and the demand can be so great you are again choosing the jobs."

The downturn has led to increased enrolments at technical schools, with laid-off workers hoping to ride out the recession by upgrading their skills and others postponing a job search with more education.

Over the past 28 years at SAIT Polytechnic, vice-president of academics Gordon Nixon said he has seen a trend of high applications when job prospects are low.

Compared with the same period last year, applications for courses have gone up 24 percent.

"Low-skilled jobs that don't require a lot of education are generally the first to have layoffs," Nixon said.

"During an economic boom, when people are making decisions like finishing high school or continuing with their education, many people don't consider education as an option."

With many of the school's programs taking two years or less, Nixon said students hope to graduate in time for an economic recovery.

That's Aubrie Basque's plan.

Right after high school, Basque got a job in retail working at a sporting goods store in a shopping mall.

In five years, she became manager and kept applying for jobs to work in administrative positions with the provincial government. And after years of trying, she recently learned she got a job in the public sector.

"It's a good time for me to leave retail and do something else," she said. "Working retail was great but it's time to try to go back to school and get a steady job in government."

Over the past six months, Basque, 24, said she's changed her spending habits and has seen customers weigh purchases more carefully.

Her leaving gives co-worker Brent Yamada, 21, a promotion to management.

Just last August, Yamada remembers a co-worker asking for and getting increased benefits and raises. Those days are gone.

"Happy to have a job," he said. "Lots of people don't."

Others, who have seen the highs and lows, are opting out of the economy altogether. Catherine O'Rourke, who moved to Calgary in 1998 before the big economic boom, left a few months ago for Regina, where the Saskatchewan economy is still on the rise.

Her condo, bought when prices were high in 2006, has dropped in value over the last year, but O'Rourke, 30, made money when she sold another condo a year earlier when the market skyrocketed. She's now selling, or hoping to swap it for a house in Regina, after getting a secure job in Saskatchewan as a legal assistant.

Her friends who are legal assistants in Calgary are facing benefit cuts and wage freezes.

"There were things I didn't notice" until after the boom faded, said O'Rourke.

"During the boom, you couldn't get good service anywhere, there was no staff. There were so many jobs out there that they had people who didn't care about customer service."

O'Rourke said she knew the boom was over when she went into a restaurant a few months ago and got served right away.

Article II

Headline: Deeley Does Harley-Davidson Distribution

On the surface, distributing products to retailers should be a simple process. Products come into a distribution centre and get put on shelves. Orders come in from the field. Products are picked, packed and shipped. However, doing it right can be an Olympian task, and conscientious distributors try to do it swifter, quicker, faster.

For Deeley Harley-Davidson Canada, figuring out how to improve the distribution process—to get the right quantity of the right products to the right retailers faster—took two years of planning and implementation, and close to a million dollars, says Buzz Green, vice president and general manager of the Concord, Ontario-based company.

And Deeley has it easy, Mr. Green adds. The company has one supplier, Harley-Davidson, 26,000 stock keeping units (SKUs), many of which are ordered on a regular basis, and only 75 customers—Harley-Davidson retailers—located in one country.

Deeley has been distributing motorcycles and accessories in Canada for 86 years. In 1973, the company secured exclusive rights to distribute Harley-Davidson bikes, parts, accessories, motor clothes and other Harley-Davidson-branded items—including coffee mugs, baby clothes, shirts, jeans, jackets, hats, barbeques and jukeboxes.

Harley-Davidson, which celebrates its hundredth anniversary this year, is one of the top 10 most recognized brands in the world and Harley-Davidson motorcycle (or Hog) owners are loyal to the brand. They like to be seen wearing clothes emblazoned with the Harley-Davidson eagle logo.

Deeley processes about 2,000 lines or unique SKUs per day, or half a million per year. Multiply that by the quantity of each SKU ordered and you have a busy distribution centre generating annual revenues "in the tens of millions of dollars," says Mr. Green.

While Deeley may only have 75 customers, they serve thousands of Harley-Davidson owners across Canada. If a part is not in stock, bike riders have to wait, or get their Hogs serviced elsewhere. Mr. Green, an avid biker, understands how other Hog owners feel when their bikes are in the shop, and he admits that Deeley was not "a best in class" distributor.

The distribution system wasn't broken, but there were problems. The Deeley warehouse was not set up efficiently and the picking process was not automated. During peak periods, Deeley had to "throw more bodies" at the problem. However, hiring untrained pickers on a temporary basis increased distribution costs and led to less accurate order fulfilment.

Shipping inequities compounded the problem, adds Mr. Green. All orders were shipped by ground transportation, unless retailers paid for airfreight. Retailers close to the Concord distribution centre received orders in a day or two; others had to wait—unless they paid the air shipment premium.

In addition, picking bottlenecks were increasing. The motorcycle industry has been experiencing double-digit growth as a new generation discovers the open road and Baby Boomers, their children leaving the nest, feel free to return to their Easy Rider ways. Many of "the come-backers," as Mr. Green calls the boomers, are buying their first Harleys.

Rather than build new distribution centres in various regions, which would spread inefficiencies across the country, Deeley decided to improve productivity by using the existing warehousing space more efficiently and automating the picking process.

Six aisles of shelving units that were spaced 14 feet apart were placed just over five feet apart so staff on order picker vehicles could pick products from two shelves at the same time. An electronic track was embedded in the warehouse floor to control the vehicle's direction based on picking sequence software. Pickers carry wireless radio frequency guns that display SKUs and quantity to be picked. Once they pick product, employees scan a barcode on the shelf and the vehicle moves on.

Picking productivity in the rearranged aisles has doubled, from 22 lines per staff hour to over 40. But Deeley did not stop there.

In space created by rearranging the shelves, Deeley installed four 12-shelf carousels that will hold about 8,000 smaller, frequently ordered products. A picker, filling eight orders simultaneously, will stand on a 20-foot table in front of the carousels. As orders are sent to the carousel software, the table automatically moves to the right product shelf level. Flashing lights indicate which product to pick and LED readouts indicated the appropriate quantity. Then LEDs indicate which of the eight order bins to place the product in, and the quantity to place in the bin. Products are scanned to ensure the order has been correctly filled.

Each shelf level has 50 faces and the carousel automatically rotates, bringing the next allotment of products to the picker. Once the products on one level are picked, the table moves automatically to the next shelf level.

If a full order is filled on the carousels, the order bin heads down a conveyer to packing and then shipping. Otherwise, it rolls down another conveyer to a picker working the aisles.

The carousel system, when fully implemented this May, will allow an employee to pick 150 lines per hour. When the carousel system is fully operational, Mr. Green says orders will be processed four or five times more productively overall.

Increased productivity means fewer temporary workers will be hired, which will improve overall accuracy. It also means faster order turn-around times. The goal, once the carousels are activated, is to ship out orders received by 2:30 pm. (local time) on the day they arrive, says Mr. Green.

The project will pay for itself in two years and Deeley is pumping much of the return on investment into a free air shipment plan for retailers outside a one-day ground shipment radius. All but eight retailers in more remote areas will receive orders the next day, says Mr. Green.

"We want to get our retailer's customers back on the road ASAP," says Mr. Green, itching to get his motor running.

Article III

For the last two years, Rajvinder Dhir has lived with leukemia. For the five-year-old boy, it has meant a life of trips to and from the hospital for chemotherapy – five days a week for the first six months, now down to once or twice a week.

The chemo treatments leave Rajvinder exhausted, and his immune system vulnerable. Rajvinder's mother, Renu Dhir, is not able to take him by public transit to the Hospital for Sick Children, a one and a half hour trip from their home in Etobicoke. However, she doesn't drive. Her husband, Ravinder Singh, does drive, but he works full-time. Even so, he took a month off work to drive his son to the hospital after Rajvinder was diagnosed with leukemia.

When Ravinder had to return to work to support the family, taxi rides loomed as an expensive option for the Dhir family.

Enter the Canadian Cancer Society and its volunteer driver program.

The Canadian Cancer Society has arranged to have volunteer drivers take cancer patients to and from hospitals for more than 40 years. Last year, the Society had more than 2,900 volunteer drivers in Ontario who drove more than 10 million kilometres taking more than 16,500 patients to and from treatments.

"The Cancer society helps when I need transportation. We have different volunteer drivers, but they are always so helpful and have a feeling for us, what we are going through," says Renu.

There is always a need for volunteers to drive people to and from treatments and about 25 percent of cancer patients who need a driver in Toronto have to be turned away, says Joan Rumack, Toronto region community outreach consultant with the Canadian Cancer Society.

Even Cancer victims with cars who are able to drive themselves to the hospital cannot do so as they may not be well enough to drive home after treatment. They may even be too sick to walk home or take public transit, so they require rides.

Over the last couple of years, the demand for drivers has increased but the number of drivers has not. The reason? "More people have entered the cancer-demographics as the baby boom generation ages," says Rumack.

Aging boomers often have their hands full, looking after elderly parents while caring for their own children or working full-time. When the kids of boomers are old enough to drive a sick parent to the hospital, they often don't have the time due to work or school obligations.

Many of the Canadian Cancer Society's volunteer drivers are retired folks, like Ralph Sybring, 73, who has been driving cancer patients, including the Dhirs, to and from hospitals for two years. Also, like Sybring, a number of drivers have had family members fall victim to cancer. Sybring, in fact, lost his sister to cancer several years ago.

Like all drivers, Sybring received some training and information on how to work with patients from the Cancer Society. He also travelled with another volunteer driver a few times to learn the ropes. "It's tough in the beginning," he says. "Navigating through the city can be difficult at times when working with patients who are, at times, understandably emotional about what they are going through."

Sybring has worked as a volunteer with young people in cadets and in church groups and enjoys the volunteer work he is doing now. "Some people I've been driving for two years and they become like family," he says.

Since Sybring is retired, has some time on his hands and loves to read or chat, he frequently drives people to the hospital and waits for them, reading or chatting with others in the waiting room. However, most drivers only take a patient to the hospital or pick one up after their treatment, often on their way to or from work.

To raise awareness of the desperate need for volunteer drivers in Toronto, the Canadian Cancer Society launched a public service announcement (PSA) campaign last February, mostly using posters in hospitals, pharmacists and other locations as well garnering some media coverage. Over 70 people have called and some of the new drivers are on the road, making for 104 drivers in Toronto. The Cancer Society is looking to add at least another 50 drivers to meet demand.

In addition to recruiting independent volunteers, the Cancer Society is looking to set up formal programs with corporations in Toronto that would see employees driving patients to or from hospitals, says Rumack. Drivers need to have a valid driver's licence, good driving record and insurance. They receive reimbursement for mileage.

Appendix II: Case Study

Full case study

SPOTLIGHT – EDUCATION

Digitizing Student Records Helps Improve Productivity and
Reduces Paper at Algonquin College

The Organization

With campuses in Ottawa, Perth and Pembroke, Algonquin College is the
largest college in eastern Ontario. However, Algonquin nurtures a friendly,
small-college atmosphere. Algonquin College offers over 100 full-time programs
and a wide selection of online and part-time programs. Its diploma, degree and
certificate programs effectively combine theory and practice – the best way to
help students prepare for careers.

The Challenge

The Algonquin College office of the registrar was not new to electronic
student records. Staff had been scanning and digitizing student records for
several years, but wanted to expand the number and types of records they used.
They also needed to improve how digital records were accessed and used, but
the department had outgrown the scanning and repository limits of its legacy
system.

In addition, the system was not payment card industry (PCI) compliant,
service calls were becoming more frequent and the supplier was becoming less
responsive. As a direct result, the department was experiencing significant
downtime and productivity inefficiencies.

The Algonquin College registrar's office has 75 people, 50 of whom need to
access student information, such as admission records, exemption information
and transcripts, as a routine part of their jobs. While the office is not paperless,
digitizing student records was helping to reduce the department's physical
footprint by minimizing the need for filing cabinets.

"If our office was to maintain and improve the space and productivity enhancements of digital records, we needed to have an improved electronic record-keeping system in place," said Marie Theriault, Manager, Scheduling and System Support.

The Process

The Algonquin College registrar's office has multifunction devices (MFDs) and copiers from Ricoh. Theriault discussed records management with her Ricoh contact, who told her about Laserfiche, a document management solution that Ricoh installs and customizes. More than 30,000 organizations worldwide use Laserfiche to streamline documents, records and business process management. With 492 customers utilizing the Laserfiche document management platform in Canada, Ricoh is the largest supplier and custom integrator of Laserfiche document management systems in the country.

Once the registrar's office agreed to have Ricoh install the new document management system, the implementation process was relatively straightforward and took less than three months. Ricoh had a hard deadline for implementation as the new system had to be in place and operational before students came back to school after Labour Day.

The Solution

Ricoh set up the document management system and used built-in utilities to customize the workflow process so the new system could capture more records in more fields more rapidly. Records access was also simplified, improving staff productivity. Before the system went live, Ricoh imported all existing digital records into the new system, which was an important part of the process.

In addition to meeting Algonquin College's immediate challenge of having an effective digital student records process, Ricoh set up the new document management system to remove any payment information from documents to be stored. This helped Algonquin College ensure their records management processes complied with privacy and security regulations for personal credit card information. Today all personal credit card data entered into their system is now automatically redacted after use so it cannot be accessed once it is no longer needed.

Although the records management system is new, it functions seamlessly to students and other stakeholders served by the registrar's office.

The Result

The new document management system at Algonquin College is easy to use in terms of getting records into the database, navigating the system and accessing information. A user-friendly Windows-based navigation system replaces cumbersome record boxes.

Ricoh provided initial training on the system to key registrar's office staff members, who trained additional staff, enabling the whole office to get quickly up to speed.

"We've had a very positive working relationship with Ricoh," said Theriault. "Any concerns were immediately addressed by Ricoh. The implementation has gone smoothly, and it's actually been fun." If staff were told they had to go back to paper records or even to the old digital system, Theriault would have a revolt on her hands. "I would retire before going back!" she added. "We would recommend Laserfiche and Ricoh, most definitely."

The registrar's office is now working with Ricoh to extend the system to include workflow for student exemptions that will automate the process of student course exemption approvals – and eliminate additional paper flow in the process.

About RICOH

Ricoh Canada Inc. is a leading provider of document solutions for Canadian Businesses. Ricoh's fully integrated hardware and software solutions help organizations share information efficiently and effectively by enabling customers to control the input, management and output of documents.

Ricoh Canada Inc. is a wholly owned subsidiary of Ricoh Corporation with its head office located in Toronto, and over 2,100 employees supporting Canadian Business nationwide.

Information about Ricoh's complete range of products and services can be accessed on the World Wide Web at www.ricoh.ca

About the Author

I was seven years old when I published my first magazine. Using a stubby pencil, I meticulously printed articles about members of my family and illustrated the articles with crayon art. I produced only one copy of the magazine, but my entire family read "The Lima News."

I had great fun doing it and words have been an important part of my life ever since ...

That's a lovely story, isn't it? However, when I want to sell myself as a writer, I strike a different tone. Just like when you are writing different genres for different audiences, you have to strike a different tone. So here's my business tone.

Based in Toronto, Ontario, Paul Lima (www.paullima.com) has worked as a professional writer and business-writing instructor for over twenty-five years. He has run a successful freelance writing, copywriting, business writing, and media relations training business since 1988.

Paul has had short stories and poetry published in numerous literary magazines and online journals and read on CBC Radio. You can read excerpts from some of his short stories at www.paullima.com/cw.

An English major from York University, Paul has worked as a copywriter, continuing education manager and magazine editor.

Additional Books by Paul Lima

Paul is the author of twelve books on writing and several other business-related topics, including:

- *How To Write A Non-Fiction Book in 60 Days*
- *Harness the Business Writing Process*
- *Everything You Wanted to Know About Freelance Writing...*
- *The Six-Figure Freelancer: How to Find, Price and Manage Corporate Writing Assignments*
- *Business of Freelance Writing: How to Develop Article Ideas and Sell Them to Newspapers and Magazines*
- *Fundamentals of Writing: How to write articles, media releases, case studies, blog posts and social media content*

- *(re)Discover the Joy of Creative Writing*
- *Unblock Writer's Block (**Note:** many the exercises in this book are similar to many of those in (re)Discover the Joy of Creative Writing)*
- *Copywriting That Works: Bright ideas to Help You Inform, Persuade, Motivate and Sell!*
- *How to Write Media Releases to Promote Your Business, Organization or Event*
- *Do you Know Where Your Website Ranks? How to Optimize Your Website for the Best Possible Search Engine Results*
- *Build A Better Business Foundation: Create a Business Vision, Write a Business Plan, Produce a Marketing Plan.*

All books and short reports are available online in print and/or digital format, from www.paullima.com/books.

For information on online courses on writing and the business of writing, visit www.paullima.com/ecourses.

CPSIA information can be obtained
at www.ICGtesting.com
Printed in the USA
BVOW08s0924300118
506496BV00003BA/99/P